By: Robert DuPrey, Ph.D.

WORK PLACE OF THE FUTURE

- ♣ Transforming Organizational Culture
- ♣ Managing Diversity
- ♣ Technological Change and Globalization
- ♣ Leadership Skills required for International Competition
- ♣ Managing Change and Risks involved
- ♣ Future Outlook

Order this book online at www.trafford.com
or email orders@trafford.com

Most Trafford titles are also available at major online book retailers.

Printed in Victoria, BC, Canada.

ISBN: 978-1-4269-2953-3 (sc)

ISBN: 978-1-4269-2954-0 (e-book)

Our mission is to efficiently provide the world's finest, most comprehensive book publishing service, enabling every author to experience success. To find out how to publish your book, your way, and have it available worldwide, visit us online at www.trafford.com

Trafford rev. 3/29/2010

 www.trafford.com

North America & international
toll-free: 1 888 232 4444 (USA & Canada)
phone: 250 383 6864 ♦ fax: 812 355 4082

WORK PLACE OF THE FUTURE

Introduction

The last quarter of this century we saw major improvements in worker safety and health in workplaces. While some problems remain, new and largely unforeseeable safety and health concerns will emerge in the workplaces of the next century. Although diminishing, employment discrimination has not been eradicated. Worker's personal health will increasingly be a workplace issue, potentially causing concern about rights to privacy. Both old and new problems present challenges and opportunities for cooperation among employers, workers, labor unions and policymakers.

New technology and growing global trade have change economy's mix of jobs and industries. Computers have revolutionized work and workplaces and raised the skill requirements for many jobs. "Employer's need for greater workforce flexibility, coupled with efforts to hold down benefit costs, will increase demand for nontraditional workers" (Herman, 1999, p. 99).

This book first reviews the history of efforts in improving workplace conditions, and analyzes the current conditions and evaluates the effects of technological changes on workers. Second, identifying the need for improving the work place and discuss the problem in managing technological change will be explored. Third, the Taylor's concept of manual work and other various methods and tools of improving work place are discussed with appropriate theoretical bases. Last, the remaining actions that should be addressed for the future of workplace are discussed, with a conclusion and recommendation and will offers a glimpse of potential future concerns.

Existing Situation and Workplace Conditions

Full-time workers typically spend more than one-third of their weekday waking hours at work. Clearly, the conditions under which they work can have a major effect on their lives. Most workers feel completely unprepared to cope with the enormity of the transition-taking place in today's organizations. "The rash of current technological breakthroughs and economic restructuring initiatives seem to have descended on workers with little warning." (Rifkin, 1995, p.101). Suddenly all over the world men and women are asking if there is a role for them in the new future unfolding across the global economy. Workers with years of education, skills, and experience face the very real prospect of being made redundant by the new forces of automation, information and globalization.

Engels (1946) write "the ever increasing perfectibility of modern machinery is turned into a compulsory law that forces the individual industrial capitalist always to improve his machinery, always to increase its productive force. The extension of the markets can not keep pace with the extension of production". The collision, he wrote, "becomes inevitable" (p. 25).   While the new information technology and robotics are changing the nature of some industries such as farm management, replacing machines for human labor in virtually every area of activity. "the new gene-splicing technologies are changing the very way plants and animals are produced. Genetic engineering is the application of engineering standards to the manipulation of genes." (Rifkin, 1995, p 118). The decline of the labor force in farms has left fewer and farms and caused high cost of machine capital and increases in the price of goods and products. Kennedy (1993) writes that "it is estimated that each robot replaces four jobs in the economy and if in constant use twenty-four hours a day, will pay for itself in just over one year." (p. 131). The challenge of putting back the workers to work and making rooms for workers will stay with leaders for many years to come.

Another area of problem is safety. Federal government recognizes the need to protect workers' safety and health. Many governmental safety acts have passed to make the work a safe and healthy place for men and woman and all employees. Today workers are healthier and more productive than ever due to the fact that they use new technology and computer systems in order to perform their duties. What is lacking is the mass of blue color workers that use to work in assembly lines and produce top quality products. They have been replaced with machines and computer technology. Another problem is lack of high skill workers in all industries, especially in technology telecommunication. "The new information and telecommunication technologies are also making office less relevant as centers of operations." (Rifkin, 1995, p. 149). Portable fax machines, modems and wireless laptop computers allow business to be conducted either on location or from home. What is though missing is the labor force to maintain the existing technologies and the shortage of managers in this field will continue for years to come.

Skill Workers

Demand for higher-skilled employees is a major problem that has become increasingly important last few years. Where strength and manual dexterity used to be enough to ensure employment and a comfortable standard of living, more jobs now and in the future will require verbal and mathematical, as well as organizational and interpersonal, skills. Emerging technologies, globalization and the information revolution are also increasing demand for high-tech skills. Workers welcome the increasing number of new job opportunities that are available in a broad spectrum of industries such as healthcare, computer technology and such. The want ads, clamoring for workers in the information technology, communications, and service industries, reflect both the increased opportunities for workers and the increased need for up-to-date skills. Workers and businesses are responding by investing in more education and training.

In the midst of the creation of these new high-tech jobs, most current jobs will endure albeit in altered form. Skills will need updating as technology introduces new ways of completing age-old tasks. For example, many classroom teachers will continue to stand before their students, while some will appear by video or satellite hook-up, on-line courses, distance leaning and answer students at night via e-mail. The fundamental skills used by these workers will endure but they will also need new skills to function effectively. There are, however, few working individuals who will not face the need for supplementary skills to remain competitive in their existing jobs.

Skill requirements have increased for many jobs in the global economy, but a closer examination reveals a more complex relationship between technology and job content. Consider the change in machine shops from manually operated machine tools, such as lathes and drilling machines, to computer-programmed machine tools. Manual operation required skill in reading gauges and other measurement devices as well as manual dexterity acquired through relatively long periods of training and doing.

Contrast this with the requirements for users of newer, computer-programmed machine tools. Newer machine tools require much less manual dexterity, but they demand computer literacy and perhaps some programming, a very different skill package.

The machine-tool operator today is more likely to insert a programmed diskette into a control module than to set measurement devices manually. The computer program itself is likely to have been written by a programmer, not by a machine-tool operator on the shop floor. Though it might appear that machine-shop workers' skill requirements have decreased, some workers may exercise discretion over the programmed tool. In fact, some jobs in the machine shop have been de-skilled while others have been redesigned to require formal education in new, abstract skills such as use of programming languages.

The occupational groups that require the most education are projected to be among the fastest growing. Employment in professional specialty healthcare occupations is projected to increase the fastest. To meet rising skill needs, young workers are raising their skills, not only by obtaining more schooling, but by participating in post-school training to a somewhat greater extent than did previous generations. According to Bowers & Swaim (1994) much of "the investment in post-school adult education is being made by workers who already have higher levels of formal educational attainment." (pp. 79-88).

Productivity

Along with efforts to improve productivity through increased worker skills, many employers are trying to improve productivity by reforming the way they organize work and motivate workers. "Work reform movements typically proceed in cycles of enthusiasm followed by disillusionment, but after trial and error, the best elements usually become part of the accepted way of doing business." (Bailey, 1993). Successful reforms will shape the workplaces of the future. To increase quality and lower costs, some companies are experimenting with greater worker involvement and interaction, through innovative work practices such as worker's teamwork. Team groups are involved in "total quality management, quality circles, peer review of employee performance, worker involvement in process decisions and job rotation." (Gittleman, Horrigan & Joyce, 1998). Labor unions often work with employers to put such concepts into practice in the workplace. "Additional practices used to boost productivity including profit sharing, linking pay to performance, decentralizing responsibility and increasing worker autonomy." (King, 1995). Changes in workplace and factory layouts may also increase efficiency and reduce ergonomic-related injuries. Such work practices can often result in high performance particularly when combined with increased training, new technology, improved communications among producers, suppliers, customers and company divisions or new tools for inventory and quality control. "Organizations that integrate several of production control approaches have been called high performance work organizations." (King, 1995).

Many workplaces where workers are represented by a union, have adopted one or more of these work practices. Companies use computers and telecommunications tools to link to customers and suppliers. Sometimes, because of these new tools, companies faced with rapidly changing market conditions rely upon the increased involvement of workers and their unions in managing the production process. Workers and their unions, often through use of teams can help management to anticipate problems and bottlenecks, participate in new product development, and monitor quality, address safety and health issues and many others.

"Many firms are experimenting with linking worker pay and company performance more directly through profit sharing." (Kruse, 1993). "Gain sharing is another type of compensation system in which pay corresponds more directly to worker performance." (Bednarzik, 1993). Some companies allow workers to buy company stock through payroll deductions at rates discounted from the market share price. These practices increase the economic stake that workers have in company performance. Limited percentage of the workforce, these direct linkages of employees to the success of their companies, if they pay off in company productivity, is likely to spread.

The effectiveness of alternative work organizations depends on appropriate human resource management. "One recent analysis mentioned that innovative work practices can improve the economic performance of a company only if three requirements are met: 1) the employees possess knowledge and skills that managers lack, 2) the employees are motivated to apply these skills and knowledge, and 3) the organization is structured to channel these skills and knowledge towards improving productivity." (Bailey, 1993). Many experiments in work organization have resulted in dramatic changes in the way companies operate. Not all will prove superior to approaches named, but those that do improve productivity are more likely to be found in the workplaces of the future.

Another factor to improve productivity is efficiency. Efficiency came to dominate the workplace and the life of modern society, in large part, because of its adaptability to both the machine and human culture. There was a time value designed to measure the input/output ratio of energy and speeds in machines that could easily be applied to the work of human beings and the workers of all of society. Within its grasp, every force and activity became instrumental to utilitarian and productive goals. From then on, human beings and machines were measured and assigned worth based on their relative efficiencies. Galbraith (1979) writes this new "technological proficiency and production efficiency as the power in the giant corporations that has passed from the stockholders to the techno-structure." (pp. 94-101). Galbraith et al. (1979) argues that "the growing complexity of the modern corporation, coupled with the introduction of increasingly sophisticated technology, required specialized talent and a new breed of scientific-minded managers who could run the institutions more like the efficient machines they were becoming." (p. 95). Another theory by Veblen (1921) who writes "envision a country run by professional engineers who, using the most rigorous standards of efficiency, would root out inefficiencies and operate the country like a finely tuned mega-machine." (pp. 120-121).

Rifkin (1995) writes that "the business community has long operated under assumption that gains in productivity brought on by the introduction of new technologies rightfully belong to the stockholders and corporate management in the form of increased dividends and larger salaries and other benefits." (p. 227). Workers claims on productivity advanced, in the form of higher wages and reduced hours of work that have generally been regarded as illegitimate and even parasitic. Their contribution to the production process and the success of the company has always been viewed as of a lesser nature than those that provide the capital and take the risk of investing in new machinery. For that reason any benefits that accrue to the workers from productivity advances are viewed not as a right, but rather as a gift bestowed by management.

With computer technology in many segments of the organizations, workers are using a shorter work hours and use of satellite office and home-based office. Economists such as Leontief (1986) were preparing the ground for the transition to the shorter workweek. Leontief (1986) argues that the mechanization of the manufacturing and service sectors is similar to what took place earlier in the century in agriculture. In the case of agriculture, the government stepped in and established an income policy to help the farmers adjust to overproduction against ineffective demand. Leontief (1982) notes that "industrial nations already have a well-established income policy for their labor forces in the form of social security benefits, unemployment benefits, medical insurance and welfare payments." (pp. 194-195). He concludes that "what is needed is a broadening of the idea of income transfer to adjust to the tightening grip of technological displacement". He suggests that "a first tentative step in that direction might include supplemental benefits to those who work less than the normal hours." (p. 195).

While economists such as Leontief et al. (1982) believe that "technological change is inevitable, they admit that the emerging knowledge sector will not be able to create enough jobs to absorb the millions of workers displaced by re-engineering and automation (....) favors a shortening of the workweek as a means of sharing the available work, but adds that it should be voluntary and not mandated, because enforcement is difficult." (pp. 194-195).

Leontief et al. (1982) also argues that "free time should be considered a part of workers income and ways must be found to encourage leisure." (p. 194). The constructive use of leisure, he further argues, "can come about only with an improvement in education." (p. 194).

Another liberal economist Theobald (1967) argues that "since automation would continue to boost productivity and replace workers, it was necessary to break the traditional relationship between income and work." (p. 19). He continues that "with machines doing more and more of the work, human beings would need to be guaranteed an income, independent of employment in the formal economy, if they were to survive and the economy were to generate adequate purchasing power for the public to buy the goods and services being produced." (p. 19). He, among other economists perceives the quarantined annual income as a turning point in the history of economic relationships, and hopes that its eventual acceptance would transform the very idea of economic thinking from the traditional notion of scarcity to the new ideal of abundance. He writes that "the guaranteed income represents the possibility of putting into effect the fundamental philosophical belief which has recurred consistently in human history, that each individual has a right to a minimal share in the production society." (pp. 19-20).

Organizational Culture

Organizational culture is defined as a system of learned, shared values, beliefs and norms that are used to interpret elements in the environment and as a guide for all kinds of behavior (Geertz, 1973). Organizational culture is not something that is found in a mission statement or corporate policy manual; rather, organization culture is communicated and reinforced through organizational mechanism (Ott, 1989). Organizational cultural interventions involve more than simply restating values, beliefs or norms and communicating them to individuals. Cultural changes involve a complex process of replacing an existing paradigm with another (DeSimone, 1998). Organizational dimensions that support a learning organization must have structure, information, leadership and human resource development practices.

One of the key dimensions of a learning organization is the removal of hierarchical barriers that divide managers and employees. In their place, learning organizations have implemented more collaborative structure like self managed teams and cross-functional teams. Senge (1990) writes "teams provide a natural setting for sharing and dissemination of information. If teams develop a learning capacity, they become a microcosm for other teams in the organization. Teams can serve as an incubator for new ideas, since their limited size and focus permit then to mobilize their resources and experiment more efficiently than larger units." New knowledge gained through team learning can be propagated to other teams or individuals, although there is no guarantee this will occur. Information acquisition and information sharing is also very important in support of learning organization. While individuals and teams can learn, solve problems and create new ideas, the organization will not have learned unless this new knowledge is acquired, stored and made available to other organizational members, both now and in the future (Gephart, 1996). Knowledge can be acquired from both internal and external sources. Internal sources would involve interactions between group members who can think insightfully about complex issues and are able to use their combined potential (Senge, 1990).

For human resource development practices, there are a number of human resource management practices that are necessary to support a learning organization. Cummings & Worley (1997) write "performance appraisal and reward systems that reinforce long-term performance and the development and sharing of new skills and knowledge are particularly important". Formal training programs developed in advance and delivered according to a preset schedule are insufficient to address shifting training needs and encourage timely information sharing. Human resource development professionals must become learning facilitators (Gephart, 1996). Gephart et al. continues on saying "Their role should be to assist, consult and advise teams on how best to approach learning. They must be able to develop new mechanisms for cross-training peers, team members and new systems for capturing and sharing information".

Organization's culture is made up of the shared beliefs, expectations and behavioral patterns that define the organization's identity to its members (Gephart et al., 1996). In a learning organization, the organizational culture contains elements that promote learning and knowledge sharing throughout the organization. One challenging fact about the organizational culture is to move individuals and groups toward a new set of expectations and norms.

Leadership role is also critical to the success of a learning organization. A leader in a learning organization is viewed by some theories and practitioners as someone who can move the organization toward the kinds of culture, systems and practices that are needed to support the concepts of learning. Senge (1996) argues that "leadership is needed not only at the top of a learning organization; it is needed at every level, especially at executive level, local line level and the internal networkers and community builders".

In order to have an organization that supports training and implement training programs, they need to be flexible to deal with change and the processes of change. Change process theory tries to explain the dynamics through which organizational improvement and changes take place (Woodman, 1989). Lewin (1958) first depicted the change process as occurring in "three stages, 1) unfreezing, 2) moving and 3) re-freezing. The unfreezing stage involves the process of getting people to accept the change as inevitable and to stop doing certain things that resist change, such as the policy, practice and behavior. The moving stage involves getting people to accept the new, desired state such as new policies and practices. The last stage, re-freezing involves making the new practices and behaviors a permanent part of the operation or role expectation".

In order for organizations to compete successfully in a global economy, they must be able to attract and retain the best employees possible. For some organizations, this may mean recruiting and hiring more women and minorities for roles that have been nontraditional for them such as management. Judy & D'Amico (1997) write, "There has been a gradual increase in the number of woman and racial and ethnic minorities such as Black, Hispanic and Asian entering the workforce. The prediction is that this trend will continue at least through the year 2020". Organizations are subsets of larger sociopolitical cultures. Relationships between the larger sociopolitical culture and organizational cultures are referred to as "cultural paradigms which tie together the basic assumptions about humankind, nature and activities" (Schein, 1987, p.264). According to Schein et al. these assumptions are the building blocks or the roots of an organizational culture.

Diversity

Cultural diversity is defined as the existence of two or more persons from different cultural groups in any single group or organization (DeSimone, 1998, p. 485). Most organizations are culturally diverse because their employees are from different cultural subgroups whether gender, race, ethnic origin. Even if an organization is culturally diverse, it may not be aware of or acknowledge the diversity (DeSimone, 1998, p. 485). It is estimated that 47 percent of organizations conducted diversity training in 1996 down 6 percent from 1995 (Industry Report, 1996). Diversity training programs vary in scope and length. At one extreme is one to three a day program for managers that are designed to transform them into culturally sensitive people. Most of these training programs are one-time programs that have no follow-up training to reinforce some of the issues.

According to Lynch, (1997) "there is some evidence suggesting that diversity training can at least make individuals aware of cultural distinction. A survey of employees who attended diversity training found that 62 percent felt the training was worthwhile in raising awareness of racial and genders differences. There were, however, most of the respondents whites, 87 percent and black, 52 percent felt that race relations were good or better in their own organization before the training". An organizational evaluation of a diversity training program at the Federal Aviation Administration (FAA) found that training made a significant difference in raising awareness (Tan, 1996). The result of a custom designed diversity training program for a power company indicates that employees had been receptive and that the training had improved how they behave toward others, both internally and externally (Mueller, 1996).

Thomas (1991) defines managing diversity as "a comprehensive managerial process for developing an environment and organizational culture that works for all employees" (p. 10). This approach goes beyond both affirmative action and valuing diversity because it focuses on building an environment for everyone and on full utilization of the total workforce. Thomas et al. (1991) indicates that " it is an attempt to create a level paying field for all employees without regards to cultural distinction". Thomas et al. writes "managing diversity requires; 1) a long-term commitment to change, 2) substantive change in organizational culture, 3) a modified definition of leadership and management roles, 4) both individual and organizational adaptation and 5) structural changes".

According to the National Trade Council (NTC) more than 250,000 U.S. citizens are working overseas (Dolanski, 1997). To prepare these individuals for their assignments, many organizations are providing cross-cultural training. Most cross-cultural awareness training programs deal with 1) raising the awareness of cultural differences, 2) focusing on ways attitudes are shaped, 3) providing factual information about each culture and 4) building skills in the areas of language, nonverbal communication, cultural stress management and adjustment adaptation skills (Callahan, 1989).

In some cases, the changing demographics of the workforce represent a challenge to human resource development professionals. One of the challenges is to eliminate all causes of treatment discrimination. Human Resource Development (HRD) professionals must be willing to confront some of the underlying assumptions, beliefs and attitudes that foster bigotry and stereotyping that exist within organization. HRD must advocate for people who are victims of discrimination and be willing to fight for institutional justice. HRD professionals should also examine their organization's practices in the areas of socialization, orientation, career development, and sexual and racial harassment.

In sum, as organizations become more global, the need for cross-cultural training must grow. Organizations must prepare employees for overseas assignments by giving them language skills and indoctrinating them in the customs, culture and laws of the host country.

Globalization Effect

The globalization of the market sector and the diminishing role of the government sector will mean that people will be forced to organize into communities of self-interest to secure their own future. Rifkin et al. (1995) writes "making a successful transition into a post-market era will depend largely on the ability of an aroused electorate, working through coalitions and movements, to effectively transfer as much of the productivity gains as possible from the market sector to the third sector, volunteer work, in order to strengthen and deepen community bonds and local infrastructures." (pp. 249-250). Only by building strong, self sustaining local communities will people in every country be able to withstand the forces of technological displacement and market globalization that are threatening the livelihoods and survival of much of the human family.

The current government and the government of the future will have to play a far different role in the emerging high tech era, one less tied to the interests of the commercial economy and more aligned with the interests of the social economy. Forging a new partnership between the government and third sector, volunteer work, to rebuild the social economy could help restore civic life in every nation. Feeding the poor, providing basic health care services, educating the nation's youth, building affordable housing and preserving the environment top the list of urgent priorities in the years head. All of these critical areas have been either ignored or inadequately attended to by the forces of the marketplace.

The government could also encourage greater participation in the third sector, volunteer groups, by providing a tax deduction for every hour of volunteer time given to legally certified tax exempt organizations. "Providing tax deductions for persons donating their time to volunteer efforts would ensure greater involvement in a range of social issues that need to be addressed. While there would be a loss of taxable revenue at the front side, it would likely be more than compensated for by a diminished need for expensive government programs to cover needs and services best handled by volunteer efforts in the third sector." (Rifkin, 1995, pp. 256-257). Paying for social income and for re-education and training programs to prepare men and women for a career of community service would require significant government funds. Some of the money could come from savings brought about by gradually replacing many of the current welfare bureaucracies with direct payments to persons performing community service work. With community organizations and non profit groups taking greater responsibility for addressing needs traditionally handled by government, more tax money would be freed up to provide community service incomes and training for the millions who would be working directly in their own neighborhood to help others.

As far as work safety, workers are better protected against workplace injuries (read "Safe Zone" by Robert DuPrey Ph.D.). Families suffer fewer work-related tragedies. Employers can focus resources on increasing their competitive positions, rather than paying workers' compensation for preventable injuries and illnesses. As we continue to learn more about chemicals and other workplace contaminants, the effects of poorly designed equipment and processes and other workplace hazards, it is clear that workers continue to suffer from injuries and illnesses that can be prevented with knowledge, attention and cooperation among governments, employers, workers and unions. There has been a marked change in the safety and health of the workforce since the enactment of the Occupational Safety and Health Act. "National Safety Council data show that the rate of decline in workplace fatalities has been more rapid since creation of the Occupational Safety and Health Administration (OSHA) within the Department of Labor." (Herman, 1999, p.35).

According to Herman (1999) "work death rates dropped by 38 percent in the 22-year period to OSHA's existence, from 29 per 100,000 workers in 1948 to 18 per 100,000 in 1970. In the 22 years following the OSH act, work death rates dropped by over 61 percent, from 18 per 100,000 in 1970 to 7 per 100,000 in 1992." (p. 36).

The work places of the future will, of course, bring new challenges. Less people than ever will work in the offices and remote virtual offices will replace traditional office space. A growing number of people around the world will be spending less time on the job and have more time on their hands. Whether their free time will be coerced, involuntary and the result of forced part-time work, layoffs and unemployment, or leisure made possible by productivity gains, shorter workweeks and better income remain to be worked out in the political arena. Rifkin et al. (1995) notes that "if massive unemployment of a kind unknown in history were to occur as a result of the sweeping replacement of machines for human labor, then the chances of developing a compassionate and caring society and a world view based on transformation of the human spirit are unlikely." (p. 248). The more likely course would be allowing workers to benefit from increases in productivity with shorter workweeks and adequate income, more leisure time will exist than in any other period of modern history. That free time could be used to renew the bonds of community and rejuvenate the democratic legacy. A new generation might transcend the narrow limits of nationalism and begin to think and act as common members of the human race, with shared commitments to each other, the community and the larger biosphere.

Technological Change

Zuboff (1988) invents the verb to informate, to describe the way information technology inserts data in between the worker and the product. The factory worker no longer manipulates the sheet of steel. Worker manipulates the data about the steel. Work that has been informated is no longer physical but is, instead, a sequence or pattern of information that can be handled and changed almost as if it were tangible. An order, once entered into a salesperson's laptop in a customer's office, becomes simply data and it automatically triggers a chain of data events with a minimum of further human intervention.

The rapid computerization and networking of American businesses, industries, and homes has been called a microprocessor revolution. That revolution is fundamentally transforming the way and the speed with which, people think, connect, collaborate, design and build, locate resources, manipulate tools, conduct research, analyze and forecast, reach markets, present themselves and their wares, move and track products, make transactions, in short, do business. Advances in the computer industry, coupled with those in telecommunications, have created the new information technology, or IT, industry and inaugurated an information age. "By 2006, nearly half of all U.S. workers will be employed in industries that produce or intensively use information technology, products, and services." (U.S. Department of Commerce projections, 1999).

The workplace and workforce impacts of these technological changes have been so pervasive, so dramatic in size and speed, as to be hard to describe. Starting in the 1950s, an entirely new industry was established, led by the large mainframe computer companies such as IBM, RCA, Honeywell, and Univac. These companies opened a host of new jobs producing, maintaining, and servicing computer systems. Computer programmers, keypunch operators, computer service technicians, and computer sales personnel were soon in demand by the tens of thousands, good jobs to support a growing industry. Yet in less than fifty years, only a relative handful of the jobs created in that initial wave of computerization still exist, held by workers servicing older systems still in operation. In their wake have come millions of still-newer jobs in an ever-widening variety of computer applications created to capitalize on the capacities of hardware and software systems. The life span of a personal computer provides one illustration of the diminishing time between introduction and obsolescence of new technologies. "The average life of a personal computer, or PC, has decreased from 4 1/2 years in 1992 to just over 3

years in 1999, and is predicted to be only 2 years by 2007."
(USA Today, 1999, p. 3A).

The information technology industry is evolving
rapidly. To understand the dynamics of the transformation
underway, it is important to grasp both the scope and the
speed of this revolution. Its roots are indeed very recent,
beginning with the widespread introduction of large
mainframe computers in the 1950s and '60s, followed by
steady advances in computing power that permitted a
decrease in their physical size. The introduction and
dramatic growth of personal computers in the 1980s took
even the computer industry by surprise, threatening the
mainframe operations of the larger companies. Computers
moved into millions of American homes.

The growth and reach of the Internet enables
virtually free communication among a large number of
people. "In 1995, there were only 22 million Internet users
in the United States. By 1998, the figure had quadrupled to
88 million. Estimates are for 110 million users in 1999 and
133 million by the year 2000 (....) it has taken only seven

years for the Internet to be adopted by 30 percent of Americans, com-pared to seventeen years for television and thirty-eight years for the telephone." (Survey Report, 1999). This dramatic growth is continuing as the information available on the Internet is growing rapidly and its utility to users is increasing. A novelty in the mid-1990s, the Web has become a household word and an indispensable tool of industry.

"The computer and IT revolutions have changed virtually every industry in the economy. Numerous examples illustrate the point:

- A manufacturing plant can be operated by a handful of technicians controlling robotic systems. According to Majedi (2010) "Human oversight will be reduced to minimum"
- State-of-the-art inventory systems can supply needed parts just in time for assembly.

- New jobs have been created in airfreight and delivery systems to service such just-in-time inventory operations.
- Handheld mobile phones have become commonplace, and digital phone systems will soon be able to reach anyone in the world via satellite. "(Herman, 1999).

Businesses have found ways to reduce the costs of carrying large inventories of intermediate parts and finished goods through computer-managed inventories and just in time manufacturing and servicing. Barcode scanners like those at store checkout counters are among the innovations that have helped businesses meet consumer demand more effectively by more closely monitoring inventories, reducing lead time for delivery of goods, and reducing inventories. Leading manufacturers have developed computer links to their suppliers and customers. Their suppliers follow progress on the production line via computer hookup and can plan on shipping parts and materials to the right place at the right time, minimizing inventories and downtime. Their customers have computer access to the latest production status and thus know precisely when to expect delivery. A major airplane manufacturer, for example, maintains a parts-distribution Web page that greatly speeds the pace at which planes are serviced. Locating a part used to take five to ten hours, often forcing cancellation of a flight; parts can now be located within minutes. Diesel-engine manufacturer's link via computer to the service records of the truck engines they have sold, permitting them to predict more precisely the demand for replacement engines. Global manufacturing companies link their design centers in different countries to create inter-national design teams.

The technological revolution has also launched entirely new industries, such as biotechnology. Literally hundreds of new companies have emerged in areas unheard of a decade ago. Advances in virology, cancer research, and neurology are being made as a direct result of advances in computational and information systems. Researchers can now use genetic mapping systems to locate the genes responsible for a variety of hereditary diseases. Emerging industries such as environmental technology benefit from applications ranging from remote sensing systems to biological agents that eat harmful chemicals or waste, applications made possible through advances in computer and information technologies.

Technology and job creations are link together. Employment patterns in the computer-manufacturing sector illustrate the complex impact of technological change on the workforce. "Computer-manufacturing jobs skyrocketed until 1984 as American producers dominated world production of all kinds of computers. Between the appearance of the first PCs in the mid-1970s and 1983, computer industry jobs in the United States grew by nearly 80 percent, while total U.S. manufacturing employment grew by only 4 percent." (Judy & D'Amico, 1997, p. 17). This dramatic growth was interrupted, however, by the entry of foreign computer producers into U.S. markets, which contributed to "a 26 percent drop in U.S. computer employment between 1983 and 1994." (Judy & D'Amico, 1997, p. 18).

The drop in computer-production jobs, however, was more than offset by growth in computer-related jobs for sales clerks, software designers, and Local Area Network (LAN) operators. This dynamic characterizes the rapidly evolving industry; significant growth in new jobs and activities masks the destruction of older jobs. This churning in employment often goes unnoticed. Downsizing, rightsizing, efficiency mergers, and buyouts are facts of life in this industry and throughout the new economy. With the continued rapid evolution of technology especially in healthcare, the cycle of job growth, destruction, and creation especially in the healthcare will also continue into the foreseeable future. The dynamics of the change may be less obvious in the future but much more widespread. In spite of the fact that recent global economy recession reduced the need for high tech job but one can pick up any newspaper and read a story about the demand for healthcare and high tech jobs, a demand reflected in the classified ads and their numerous listings for healthcare computerized administrators, computer specialists, Enterprise Resource Planning (ERP) package programmers, database administrators, Web designers, and so on.

Yet many jobs often require much more than the latest high-tech skills. What may not show up in the text of a classified ad is that the content of these high-tech jobs is changing. More employers want computer specialists to be knowledgeable about the industry their business is in, in addition to being technically skilled. What all of these jobs have in common is the high level of technological skills needed to perform them. Large or small, employers are no longer satisfied with an office worker who is good with figures or detail oriented. Administrative staff must now be familiar with word-processing suites, accounting and billing software, human resources packages that are computer-based and 12-to-24-line phone systems that provide call forwarding, voice mail, and conference bridges.

Old school auto mechanics can forget about getting a job if they lack the skills to use computer-based diagnostic tools now standard in repair shops. And travel agents who cannot adroitly make travel arrangements using an automated system may soon find themselves relegated to hand-delivering airline tickets. Even doctors and lawyers use technology every day for research, record keeping, or simply to communicate with colleagues and clients. As the tools of each trade become more sophisticated, many more occupations will have tech elements. Most workers will need basic computer skills to enter their chosen occupations and additional specialized training in field-specific applications to advance. It will indeed be a world that rewards lifelong learning.

The overall employment picture in high-tech industries is extremely bright both in government and private sector. "High technology has added over one million jobs to the U.S. economy since 1993." (Platzer, 1999). "Real average wages in these industries have increased 19 percent from 1990 to 1997, com-pared with a 5 percent average increase across the private sector. The average high-tech job today pays 78 percent more than the private-sector average." (Report, 1997). Technology is revolutionizing the way we work and live. Over the century, mass-production occupations have been steadily replaced by office-worker and service-provider occupations. Indeed, virtually all of the jobs that were lost in goods production and distribution "since 1969 have been offset by office jobs." (Atkinson & Court, 1998, p.9). Rather than industrial machinery, these workers' tools are telephones, fax machines, and personal computers. With the rapid introduction of mobile phones, laptops, e-mail, and the Internet, the traditional time and space requirements of office workers are no longer the rigid constraints of the past. In particular, the growth in computer applications and the Internet has enormous potential to help lower barriers to job opportunity for workers with disabilities.

A beginning trend in the increased use of flextime and flex-place followed the lifting of traditional constraints. Only a fraction of employers currently avail themselves of such arrangements, but new technologies that permit this flexibility have been introduced relatively recently: access to the Internet, widespread use of e-mail, and the prevalence of cellular and digital phones all occurred in the latter half of the 1990s. As the popularity of these tools grew, their costs decreased. Prevalence has demystified their use, making them ordinary implements for conducting business. Because the new technology is flexible, the workplace of the future will see a substantial increase in the number of workers who work from their homes or some location other than the office, though the overall proportion of workers who do so will remain small in the near future.

Assisted technologies are opening up the workplace to individuals with disabilities. Character readers and voice recognition devices, for example, help workers with visual impairments. Most people with significant disabilities are not employed, despite the fact that many have relevant labor market skills and the booming economy of the 1990s has left employers facing a severe labor shortage. Technology is bringing more people with disabilities into the workplace by removing at least some of the physical and communication barriers that have historically forced isolation and segregation. To better meet the employment needs of its agencies and of people with disabilities, as well as to further its role as a model employer, the federal government has made significant investments in providing the employment supports necessary to hire and maintain employees with disabilities. "Assisted technologies are technical accommodations, including large-screen monitors, voice-recognition software, alternative keyboards, Braille displays and printers, and other tools, that make computer and telecommunications systems accessible to employees with disabilities."(On-line). Computer Accommodation Program (CAP) provides a number of other disability-related services. "The program funds sign-language interpreters, readers, and personal assistants for employees with disabilities who need to attend long-term training; provides accurate and timely needs assessments; and hosts the CAP Technology Evaluation Center (CAPTEC), where employees and their managers can explore alternative accommodations at workstations equipped with a wide variety of assisted technologies. " (On-line). People seeking solutions to accessibility problems can visit CAPTEC to see and compare the types of equipment available. Thus customers are assured that they purchase the product most effective at helping the employee carry out his or her job. Smart prostheses employing microprocessors help their wearers to perform workplace tasks. Communications and computers make possible accommodations such as home-based work, flexible schedules, and job sharing. Home-based customer–call-in centers are examples of businesses that, because of advances in technology, have been able to tap the abilities of workers with disabilities.

New flexibility in the workplace presents a number of opportunities and challenges. Telecommuting and flex-place programs will reduce commuting time, creating more family time, allowing workers to live in areas far from their employers' offices. These new work options particularly benefit workers facing child-rearing and eldercare responsibilities and workers with disabilities. But the flexibility also opens up the possibility of exploitation and abuse if employers require homework above and beyond normal working hours or establish modern home sweatshops. Workers physically isolated from their coworkers and supervisor may also encounter a kind of discrimination, in promotions or other workplace opportunities, based on lack of face time with senior officials.

Rifkin (1995) writes "the effect of technological change is amplified by the very strategies that organizations currently use to cope with the change. Because leaders have to make decisions more quickly, organizations are shortening their chains of command, flattening their hierarchies, handing the authority for many decisions to frontline employees." (p. 17). Because organizations and leaders want to speed up production of goods and delivery of services, they turn over the redesign of their processes to cross-trained and self-managing teams of technology experts. This changes not only what is done but also who has the power to determine what will be done. Another reason is that organizations want to unburden themselves of big, slow moving inventories; they shift to just-in-time systems of materials handling which, changes procedures and processes throughout the organization. Other reason for reactions to change of technology is that many organizations want to involve their suppliers more closely in operations; they put suppliers and sometimes customers on their product development teams which, forces individuals from different functions work together as a team and that are a change for everyone who is involved.

Bridges (1994) writes "technology renders jobs obsolete by replacing the relatively slowly changing world of things with the much more mercurial world of data." (p. 14). Things have to be assembled or processed from raw materials by teams of workers; data are typed into a terminal by a single worker, or even handwritten on or spoken into tomorrow's computers. The new information and communication technologies have both increased the volume and accelerated the flow of activity at every level of society. The compression of time requires quicker responses and faster decision making to remain competitive. In the emerging nanosecond culture, the traditional control and coordination functions of management are woefully slow and utterly incapable of responding, in real time, to the speed and volume of information coming into the organization. In the information era, time is the critical commodity, and corporations bogged down by old-fashioned hierarchical management schemes can not hope to make decisions fast enough to keep up with the flow of information that requires resolution.

Today, a growing number of companies are deconstructing their organizational hierarchies and eliminating more and more middle management by compressing several jobs into a single process. They are then using the computer to perform the coordination functions previously carried out by many people often working in separate departments and locations within the company. According to Loveman (1988) "the restructuring of the corporation is fast eliminating middle management from the organizational chart" (pp. 46-65). He points out that "while better jobs are being created for a fortunate few at the top levels of management, the men and woman in garden variety middle management jobs are getting crucified by corporate re-engineering and the introduction of sophisticated new information and communication technologies." (pp. 46-65).

Departments create divisions and borders that inevitably slow down the decision making process. Companies are eliminating those borders by reassigning personnel into networks or teams that can work together to process information and coordinate vital decisions, thus bypassing the long delays that invariably accompany the shuffling of paper reports and memoranda between various divisions and levels of authority. The computer has made all of this possible. Now, any employee at any location within the company can access all of the information being generated and directed through the organization.

Companies across the globe are discovering countless new ways to use re-engineering to compress time and reduce labor costs. Increasingly, computers are providing needed information and helping to structure the coordination and flow of activity in the economic process, eliminating the need for salespersons, account executives, truck drivers, warehouse handlers, shipping department personnel and billing department people. While the new information and telecommunication technologies are eliminating jobs at every rung of the corporate hierarchy, the impact on middle management has been particularly unsettling to many in the business community. Authors Davidow & Malone (1992) sum up the growing consensus. They note that "computers can gather most information more accurately and cost effectively than people. They can produce summaries with electronic speeds and they can transmit the information to decision-makers at the speed of light." (p. 126). They continue on saying that "most interesting is that frequently this information is so good and the analysis so precise that an executive decision is no longer required." (p. 126). A well-trained employee dealing directly with the situation can now make the decision faster and in a more responsive fashion than the remote manager can miles away.

With an increasing number of workers being displaced by new laborsaving technologies and with production soaring, the business community desperately searched for new ways to reorient the psychology of existing wage earners, to draw then into what Cowdrick (1927) calls "the new economic gospel of consumption." (p.208). Workers are being swept up into a powerful new technology revolution that offers the promise of a great social transformation, unlike any in history. The new high technology revolution could mean fewer hours of work and greater benefits for millions. For the first time in modern history, large numbers of human beings could be liberated from long hours of labor in the formal marketplace, to be free to pursue leisure time activities. The same technological forces could, however, as easily lead to growing unemployment and a global depression. Whether a utopian or dystopian future awaits us depends on how the productivity gains of the Information Age are distributed.

A fair and equitable distribution of the productivity gains would require a shortening of the workweek around the world and a concerted effort by central governments to provide alternative employment in the third sector, the social economy and volunteers, for those whose labor is no longer required in the marketplace. "If the dramatic productivity gains of the high tech revolution are not shared, but rather used primarily to enhance corporate profit, to the exclusive benefit of stockholders, top corporate managers and the emerging elite of high tech knowledge workers, chances are that the growing gap between the haves and the have-nots will leads to social and political upheaval on a global scale" (Rifkin, 1995, pp. 283-289).

International Competition

Competition has placed a premium on workers globally who are educated and highly skilled. Even if future labor markets are not as tight as those today, there is every reason to believe that the workplace changes that created today's demand for skilled workers will continue. Workers with post–high-school education and training will have ample opportunities in the workplaces of the future.

The need for skilled workers will be reinforced by continuing changes in how companies and other organizations operate, such as use of work teams and increased worker autonomy. Employers of the future will place increasing value on workers who not only can operate the tools of tomorrow, but who also can find ways to increase their company's productivity and earnings.

As the workplaces of the future respond to technological change and global competition, as well as the needs of workers, the use of nontraditional employees, such as contingent workers, independent contractors, and employees of temporary help agencies, will likely rise. With the increase in these staffing arrangements, continued attention is needed to ensure that these workers receive worker protections. Additionally, these workforce trends may result in declining job stability. Workers must be ready to manage the changes and dislocations they may face by keeping their skills up to date.

In the future, scientists hope to humanize their machines, creating lifelike computer-generated images of human faces that can converse with the user from a video display screen. "By the end of the first half of the twenty-first century, scientists believe it will be possible to create life-size holographic images of computer-generated human beings capable of interacting with real human beings in real time and space." (Rifkin, 1995, pp. 143-154).

Rapid changes in technology are expected to continue especially in the healthcare sector, as is the resulting widespread impact on industries, businesses, and workers. These technological changes will further alter how products and services are made and delivered and will continue to affect the workplaces in which they are conceived, sold, and produced. The workforce of the future will need to adapt to the rapid pace of technological change by continuing to upgrade their skills. The importance of lifelong learning cannot be overestimated.

Some workers may lose their jobs as a result of changes in trade patterns. The proper public policy response to such job loss is not protectionism, but rather assisting individual workers to adjust to labor market changes caused by increased trade and globalization. The Trade Adjustment Assistance Program (TAAP) and the North American Free Trade Agreement (NAFTA) Transitional Adjustment Assistance Program, both administered by the Department of Labor, offer a comprehensive array of income support, retraining, and reemployment services to workers who lose their jobs because of international trade. Additional assistance to dislocated workers is available through the Job Training Partnership Act, which is being replaced by the Workforce Investment Act. Job search allowances may also be provided to workers seeking suitable employment outside their normal commuting area and relocation allowances may help defray moving expenses should they find employment in another part of the country.

More broadly, policies to prevent job loss from international trade or to facilitate the transition of affected workers to new jobs continue to be important. Ensuring fair and open trade among countries must remain a part of this policy package. Policies that encourage more private sector training of workers before they lose their jobs might also be an important part of a job-loss-prevention strategy.

Knowledge Worker Skills

The knowledge workers are a divers group united by tier use of state-of-the-art information technology to identify process and solve problems. They are the creators, manipulators, and purveyors of the stream of information that makes up the postindustrial, post service global economy. Their ranks include research scientists, design engineers, civil engineers, software analysts, biotechnology researchers, consultants, healthcare administrators, financial and tax consultants, architects, strategic planners, marketing specialists, film producers and editors, art directors, publishers, writers, editors and journalists. Drucker (1993) warns his business colleagues that "the critical social challenge facing the emergent information society is to prevent a new class conflict between the two dominant groups in the post-capitalist society: knowledge workers and service workers." (p. 27).

Another note from Drucker (1999) is that "the most important and indeed the truly unique, contribution of management in the 20th century was the productively of the manual worker in manufacturing. The most important contribution management needs to make in the 21st century is similarly to increase the productivity of knowledge work." (pp. 135-142). The first man to write about manual work theory and manual workers concept and study them was Taylor (1856-1915). Taylor writes,

> The first step in making the manual worker productive is to look at the task and to analyze its constituent motions. The next step is to record each motion, the physical effort it

takes and the time it takes. Then motions that are not needed can be eliminated and whenever he has looked at manual work he has found that a great many of the traditionally most hallowed procedures turn out to be waste and do not add anything. Then each of the motions that remain as essential to obtaining the finished product is set up so as to be done the simplest way, the easiest way, the way that puts the least physical and mental strain on the operator, the way it requires the least time. Then these motions are put together again into job that is in a logical sequence. (pp. 136-137)

Taylor (1892) shows that in manual work there is no such thing as skill. There are only simple, repetitive motions. What makes the worker productive is knowledge that is the way the simple, unskilled motions are put together, organized and executed. In fact, Taylor was the first person to apply knowledge to work. Drucker (1999) mentions,

"There are six factors determining knowledge worker productivity:

1- Knowledge worker productivity demands that we ask the question: What is the task?

2- It demands that we impose the responsibility for their productivity on the individual knowledge workers themselves. Knowledge workers have to manage themselves. They have to have autonomy.

3- Continuing innovation has to be part of the work, the task and the responsibility of knowledge workers.

4- Knowledge work requires continuous learning on the part of the knowledge worker, but equally continuous teaching on the part of the knowledge worker.

5- Productivity of the knowledge worker is not, at least not primarily, a matter of the quantity of output. Quality is at least as important.

6- Finally, knowledge worker productivity requires that the knowledge worker is both seen and treated as an asset rather than a cost. It requires that knowledge workers want to work for the organization in preference to all other opportunities." (pp. 142-143).

In some knowledge work and especially in some work requiring a high degree of knowledge, and management measures quality. Management mainly judgments rather than measures regarding the quality of a great deal of knowledge work. The difficulty would be to define the task and what it should be. It requires the difficult, risk-taking and always-controversial definition as to what results are for a given enterprise and given activity. Productivity of the knowledge worker will almost always require that the work itself be restructured and be made part of a system.

Re-engineering and the new information technology allow companies to collapse layers of management and place more control in the hands of knowledge worker and empower them to do self work or work in a team at the point of production. Even the effort to solicit the ideas of knowledge workers on how to improve performance is designed to increase both the pace and productivity of the plant or office and more fully exploit the full potential of the employees. Some critics, like German social scientist Dohse (1985) contend that "Japanese lean production is simply the practice of the organizational principles of Fordism under conditions in which management prerogatives are largely unlimited." (pp. 115-146)

Organizations have become increasingly dependent on skilled technical and professional employees. According to the Bureau of Labor Statistics, the fastest growing occupations between 1994 and 2005 will include those involving professionals and technical and service workers (Judy & D'Amico, 1997). This trend can be traced to changes in the workplace resulting from introduction of new technology, changing organizational goals, restructuring and reengineering. These changes include the need for more cognitive skills such as problem solving and decision-making skills and also interpersonal skills such as teamwork. Whether the changes result from plant modernization, computerization or other innovations, they have helped create a shift away from jobs requiring low-skill levels to job demanding higher skill levels. Basic skills or literacy education refers to training that focuses on upgrading reading, writing and computation skills needed to function on the job. Technical training refers to training that involves the process of upgrading a wide range of technical skills, such as computer skills needed by virtually everyone in an organization. Interpersonal skills training refer to the training that focuses on an individual's relationships with others, including communication and teamwork.

Dole (1990) writes "a major problem facing employers today is the skills gap, the difference between skill requirements of available jobs and the skills possessed by applicants." The skills gap is the result of a few factors such as the declining skill level achieved by many high school and college graduates or the growing number of racial minorities and non-English speaking immigrants in the labor market and the increased sophistication of jobs due to increased reliance on information technology (Steck, 1992).

Computer-skills training have become one of the most popular types of training. One recent survey found that 88 percent of companies conduct computer-skills training and the average company spends 25 percent of its training budget on it (Industry Report, 1996). Introductory computer training programs are used to introduce trainees to compute hardware and software. Introductory training programs focus primarily on mastering basic software application such as how to navigate the operating system through the use of manuals and tutorials that provides hands-on interactive learning. On the other hand, computer software application training covers specific software application available within an organization and instruction on applications development (Hall-Sheehy, 1985). Unlike introductory courses, which can be offered to an entire organization, application training is typically provided on an as-needed basis. With the availability of on-line capabilities of an Intranet, employees can access company's on-line computer training at any time of the day.

According to DeSimone (1998) "when organization introduces new technology by modernizing plants or computerizing operations, they typically need to update the skills of the workers who must use it." (p. 258). He continues "organizations often do this through job specific technical skills and knowledge training programs" (p. 258). A survey found that technical skills and knowledge training is conducted by 85 percent of organizations and new methods and procedures training by 78 percent (Industry Report, 1996). The goal for the lowest level of training is to prepare entry-level employees to perform basic functional responsibilities. These programs are similar to basic skill programs and combine classroom instruction with on the job training programs.

Safety training programs are another important factor in organizations. Is it estimated that 68 percent of organizations conduct some form of safety training

(Industry Report, 1996). The need for safety training has increased dramatically since the passage of the 1970 Occupational Safety and Health Act (OSHA). OSHA regulations cover four areas: 1) establishing safety standards, 2) conducting safety inspections, 3) granting safety variances for organizations that are unable to comply with standards and 4) citing organizations where standards are being violated (DeSimone, 1998, p. 253). DeSimone et al. (1998) continues "if an organization is cited for safety violation, safety training may be required to prevent future accidents." (p. 259). OSHA mandated safety-training focuses on equipment safety device, handling of toxic chemicals, safe work habits and actions to be taken in case of an accident. OSHA also has the power to levy fines, shut down an operation or prosecute the management or the owner of an organization when safety regulations are not followed.

Another important training is quality training. A critical step in developing a quality-training program is for top management to agree on what quality means to the organization and customers and on a set of metrics for measuring it. The Total Quality Management (TQM) philosophy argues that this should be done with input from people throughout the organization, especially frontline workers, and from the customers and clients the organizations serves. Quality can be defines from many perspectives including product quality, service quality and customer quality (Miller, 1992).

Another outgrowth of the quality movement was the establishment of the International Standards Organization (ISO) in 1987. The ISO's primary purpose was to establish and monitor a set of quality standards that would serve as a common reference point for international trade (Reimann & Herts, 1996). One of the ISO 9000 requirements has to do with an organization's quality training practices. DeSimone et al. writes "these requirements are 1) focuses on how the organization identifies the training needs of employees who have a direct impact on quality and 2) requires documentation of the training provided." (p. 263). ISO standards require that the organization conduct a job analysis to update the job description including the qualifications needed to perform the work.

Customer service managers need training in how to coach employees and enforce new customer service standards. Desatnick (1987) suggests that "developing a customer oriented workforce requires that hiring of service managers to train, develop and motivate employees." Organizations should provide training to service managers to ensure they understand their roles and the need to monitor and reinforce customer service standards.

Team works and cross training is two important factors in organization. A team is defined as a group of individuals who see themselves and who are seen by others as a social entity, who are embedded in one or more larger social systems such as community or organization and who perform tasks that affect others such as customers and coworkers (Guzzo & Dickson, 1996. Pp. 308-309). According to DeSimone et al. (1998) "a common form of team training is called team building. Team building refers to a collection of techniques that are designed to build the trust, cohesiveness, and mutual sense of responsibility that make for an effective team." (p. 167). Most team building interventions are led by a facilitator whose role is to help the team improve its ability to work together effectively, communicate better, improve problem solving capabilities and make better decisions.

Drucker (1999) writes "knowledge worker's responsibility for their own contribution and the knowledge worker's decision what he or she should be held accountable for in terms of quality and quantity, in respect to time and cost. Knowledge workers have to have autonomy and that entails responsibility" (p. 146).

In sum, the need for skilled and technical workers is on the rise. Employers are complaining that many young adults are graduating from schools lacking the skills needed to perform their current job. On the other hand, in many professions, professional workers are required to participate in continuing education in order to gain or renew a license or certification. Continuing education opportunities are offered by a variety of providers, including colleges and universities, professional associations and the organizations that employ professional workers.

It is often said that an organization is only as good as its people. Organizations of all types and sizes, including schools, retail stores, government agencies, restaurants and manufacturers have at least one thing in common: they must employ competent and motivated workers. This need has become even stronger as organizations grapple with the challenges presented by a fast paced, highly dynamic, increasingly global economy. To complete and thrive, many organizations are including employee education, training, and development as an important and effective part of their strategy. "It has been estimated that education and training programs accounted for as much as 26 percent of the increase in U.S. production capacity between 1929 and 1982." (Carnevale & Gainer, 1989).

Factories made it possible to increase production by using machines, computer technologies and robots and skilled workers, but they also created a significant demand for the engineers, machinists, and skilled workers to design, build and repair the machines. Fueled by the rapid increase in the number of factories, the demand for skilled workers soon outstripped the supply of vocational school graduates. In order to meet this demand, factories created mechanical and machinist training programs which were referred to as "factory schools." (Pace, Smith & Mills, 1991).

Leadership Skills

Leadership has been one of the most heavily researched and popularly discussed topics in management. There is a widespread belief that leadership skills are essential to effective management, especially for organizations that are trying to implement changes. One widely used approach to leadership training is Leader Match training that has overcome leadership training problems (DeSimone, 1998, p. 423). The program is based on a theory about what leadership is and how it can be acquired. It has also been the subject of empirical research and is backed by some evidence that it can improve one's leadership effectiveness. Leader Match training (Fiedler & Chemers, 1984) is based on the notion that effective leadership occurs when there is a match between the leader's style and the situation he or she faces. The theoretical foundation for the program is Fiedler's contingency theory of leadership. Fiedler (1964) believes that "each person has a particular leadership style based on his or her needs that dictates how he or she will act. Because this style is based on the leader's needs, it is very difficult for the leader to change it." According to Fiedler et al. (1964) "that style will not be effective in all situations. It is therefore the leader's task to diagnose the situation and either place himself in a situation favorable to his style or modify the situation so that it becomes favorable to his style".

All leaders, whether in manufacturing, service, medical, legal, education, or government, know that enthusiastic, contented employees add directly to quality, productivity, and the bottom line of profitability. Keeping employees charged up and contributing team members in a competitive marketplace is more than just pay and benefits. They must be well led. They must feel that they are valued members of the company team. Employees who feel that they are not part of the team or that their leaders don't care about their ideas are apt to be looking for what they perceive to be a better working environment. Business can ill afford to spend valuable training time and dollars on unhappy employees who leave for a better environment.

Keeping good, well-trained employees and knowing how to weed out the unproductive ones is a leadership challenge at all levels. It is not uncommon to find companies where senior leaders, due to the increasing pressures of their positions, are out of touch with the work force. The result of these problems is conflict. Conflict in itself is not necessarily negative. Without some degree of conflict, we would not continue to grow and have positive change in our organizations. It is how conflict is handled that is important. Improperly handled conflict leads to disgruntled employees, lower productivity, quality degradation, and eventually, lower profits. The ability to deal with conflict in a productive manner is one that can and must be developed in all leaders. Most businesses do not spend adequate time or effort developing their leaders at all levels. Leaders should accept the need and proceed quickly to train employees on new equipment. Improved procedures get immediate training time to ensure that everyone is on board.

Workers continuously should be trained to improve safety and to comply with regulatory requirements and standards. These activities are all-important and necessary to remain competitive and to protect work force. Leadership training below senior management level often does not get the attention that it deserves.

Mitchiner (2000) writes "senior management often attends conferences on innovative leadership techniques; however, they often fail to realize the benefit derived from training those primarily responsible for seeing that directions from that top leadership are implemented as intended, and that everyone's job is accomplished efficiently." (p. 10). Additionally, many companies promote good workers to leadership positions as a result of their performance at their current level with no leadership training for their new position. It is then wondered why such a good worker cannot handle his/her new responsibility and there is surprise when this new leader does not perform as well as was expected in the new role.

In sum, few are born with great leadership skills, but with proper training, all can be developed. Leadership itself is not complicated although some leadership theories seem to be. Leadership is simply the art of dealing with people. Leadership is made too complicated by the belief that memorizing theories, working charts and graphs, collecting unusable data, or reading the latest how to book will automatically transfer itself to skill. Some leaders bend over backward trying to befriend workers while letting organizational standards slip. Still others take the authoritarian role. None of these approaches within themselves are likely to endear a leader to those he/she is privileged to lead nor is it likely to produce quality teamwork.

Management of Change

Rifkin (1995) refers to Drucker (1993) article that writes "rapid knowledge-based change imposes one clear imperative; every organization has to build the management of change into its very structure." (p. 26). Regardless of the industry, occupation, or business, new technologies can create new problems for business and organizations in 21st century as well as new solutions. Mechanization of coal mining, for example, brought higher levels of respirable dust, creating greater potential for cases of silicosis and black lung disease but fewer injuries from accidents such as mine collapses. Workers in other settings experience analogous problems. Closed office buildings and modern cooling and ventilation systems allow for comfortable working conditions but they also contribute to indoor air quality problems ranging from Legionnaires' disease to illness caused by second-hand tobacco smoke. Computer-chip manufacturing may expose workers to many exotic chemicals whose long-term impact on workers is not yet known. These are a few examples of the health and safety issues needing attention, by employers, workers, and government, as work environments change and new technologies emerge.

A quarter of century ago, Anshen (1969) write an article in which he argued that the "accelerating dynamics of technologies, markets, information systems, and social expectations of business performance were beginning to undermine any kind of organizational design that encouraged a built-in bias in favor of the status quo". He writes:

> The single organization pattern that is free from this built-in bias is the project cluster. Project-oriented structures offer the important advantages of tailor-made design to fit unique tasks, flexible resource commitments, defined termination points and an absence of enduring commitment that encourage resistance to innovation.

Every change creates new needs. It is important to understand the fact that because the more obvious effect of change is to destroy old opportunities. For many organizations the change is their enemy and if they could the change earlier, simply relocates the opportunity by

changing customers' needs and the terms under which
success is possible, and then change can be managed
especially if leaders could so quickly to recognize this truth.
Bridges (1994) writes that "change creates opportunities in
at least four ways;

1- Needs for opening up gaps,

2- Create new interfaces,

3- New technological economic

4- Rendering obsolete." (pp.67-73).

Needs for Opening up Gaps

As change occurs, gaps open up between areas that
used to be covered by existing services and products. An
example of the gap opening is when a company is going
public and that creates the need for shareholder's service
coordinator. Another gap example is when an organization
is downsizing. That creates needs for people who can do
two or three different kinds of activities.

Create New Interfaces

Bridges (1994) writes "interface is its three-dimensional equivalent, and it captures much better the way in which whatever is on the other side" (p.69). Today organizations are entering markets unfamiliar cultural norms determine what is desirable, where diversity is increasing and being encouraged and where cross functionality are becoming the norms. One example is the new technology. Technology creates new interfaces both between different technologies and between unsophisticated workers. Technology companies are trying to build an answer to the problem of interfaces into the technology itself and encouraging knowledge workers to fill the gap and translate, interpret, train and link bridges in order to make the new technologies friendlier at workplace.

New Technological Economic

As mentioned above, technology itself creates needs and requires workers to learn new technologies, equipments and operation. The new knowledge workers are a diverse group united by their use of state-of-the-art information technology to identify process and solve problems at workplace. They are the creators, manipulators and purveyors of the stream of information that makes up the post-industrial, post-service global economy.

Rendering Obsolete

The faster product change, the faster they become obsolete, and even obsolescence creates openings and opportunities. An example of this is the Personal Computer systems that are fast changing more than all other computer systems. New products require new dimension of learning and operating and that could create opportunities for knowledge workers to be able to be flexible to deal with the change and the new opportunity that may exist.

The new economic realities of the 21st century make it far less likely that either the marketplace or public sector will once again be able to rescue the economy from increasing technological unemployment and weakened consumer demand. Information and telecommunication technologies threaten a loss of tens of millions of jobs in the years ahead in all industries and the steady decline of work in many industries and employment categories. The technological optimists counter that the new products and services of the high technology revolution will generate additional employment, and point to the fact that earlier in the century the automobile made the horse and carriages obsolete but generated millions of new jobs in the process. Although it is true that many of the products and services of the Information Age are making older products and services obsolete, they require far fewer workers to produce and operate. An example of that is the highly touted information superhighway, a revolutionary new form of two–way communications that can bring a range of information and services directly to the consumer, bypassing traditional channels of transportation and distribution. The new data superhighway (that was introduced by President Clinton and his Vise President Al Gore) will employ an increasing number of computer scientists, engineers, programmers, specialists, analysts, and writers from global market and enable them to program, monitor and run the networks. Nonetheless, their numbers will pale in contrast to the millions of employees in the wholesale and retail sectors whose jobs will be made redundant and irrelevant by the new medium.

"The few good jobs that are becoming available in the new high tech global economy are in the knowledge sector." (Rifkin, 1995, p. 283). It is native to believe that large numbers of unskilled and skilled blue and white collar workers will be retrained to be physicists, computer scientists, high level technicians, business consultants, lawyers, accountants, and the like. To begin with, the gap in education levels between those needing jobs and the kind of high tech jobs available is so wide that no retraining programs could hope to adequately upgrade the educational performance of workers to match the kind of limited professional employment opportunities that exist.

Some of the most dramatic breakthroughs in technology and engineering are occurring in the automotive, steel industries. "Post-Fordism has rapidly transforming the automobile industry and resulting in massive layoffs of blue-collar workers on the assembly line. Robots were becoming increasingly attractive as a cost-cutting alternative to human labor." (Wallace, 1989, p. 366). Wallace et al.(1989), a sociologist, writes that "the goal is to approach, as closely as possible, the human capabilities to process environment data and to solve problems, while avoiding the problems such as absenteeism and turnover, presented by human agents." (p. 366).

The steel industry fortunes were so closely linked to those of the automotive industry that it is not surprising to see the same sweeping changes in organization and production taking place in steel as are occurring in the car business. The steel industry has been the heart and soul of industrial power. The technological changes taking place in the healthcare, banking and insurance industries are indicative of the kinds of sweeping reforms that are redefining every aspect of white collar and service work. At the heart of these changes is the transformation of the traditional office from a paper handling to an electronic processing operation. The paperless electronic office has now become a goal of modern business. "The changes in office technologies and operations over the course of the Industrial Revolution have been extraordinary. The blotting paper, pencils with erasers and steel pens were introduced less than 150 years ago. Carbon paper and the keyboard typewriter were first introduced into offices in the 1870s. The keyboard calculator and punch card tabulator followed in the late 1880s. The mimeograph was invented 1890." (Beniger, 1986, pp. 280-284).

The new information and telecommunication technologies are also making offices less relevant as centers of operations. Portable fax machines, modems and wireless laptop computers allow business to be conducted either on location or from home. Telecommunications not only increased employee's productivity, but also reduces the amount of office space necessary to conduct business. While the office is being revolutionized by intelligent machines, so too is every other area of the service economy. The changes have been dramatic in the wholesale and retail sectors. Wholesalers, like middle management, are becoming increasingly redundant in the age of instant electronic communication. The new information technologies allow retailers and manufacturers to come together in a single continuous flow process, leaving little need for wholesalers. Retail establishments are also quickly re-engineering their operations, wherever possible, introducing intelligent machines to improve productivity and reduce labor cost.

In many restaurants, computer systems allow waiters to transmit orders electronically, avoiding unnecessary trips back to the kitchen. The same electronic transmission can be used by the computer to prepare a check for the customer and alert the store manager or supplier to replenish the stocks being depleted. Automated order taking, check preparation and inventory stocking significantly reduce labor requirements.

Intelligent machines are already invading the professional disciplines and even encroaching on education and the arts, long considered immune to the pressures of mechanization. Doctors, lawyers, accountants, business consultants, scientists, architects and others regularly use specially designed information technologies to assist them in their professional endeavors.

Discrimination in the Workplace

As recently as 30 years ago, classified ads for employment were divided, men wanted in one section and women wanted in another. It was unusual to see women or minorities as television news anchors and there were far fewer woman and minorities in jobs as supervisors, firefighters, police officers doctors and college professors. "Since the passage of the Civil Rights Act of 1964, minorities and woman have made real economic progress. Their wages and employment rates are up." (Herman, 1999, p. 209). Women are far more able to contribute to their families' incomes, and have become a major force in business and political life.

The black middle class is growing. "Hispanics and newer immigrant populations are emerging as strong contributors to the U.S. economy." (Herman, 1999, p. 209). A generation of professionals now provides role models for young woman and minority youths. The evidence is clear that discrimination and exclusion persist in the workplaces of today. According to U.S. Equal Employment Opportunity Commission, "there have been 12,500 claims of discrimination filed with the agency based on race/color, national origin, gender, religion, age, or disability were found to be meritorious allegations or were resolved in favor of the complaining party. In addition, it is not possible to know in how many instances other attitudes, such as discrimination based on sexual orientation, have not been remedied because current law does not reach them." (Report, date not known).

Discrimination in hiring is a continuing problem, as demonstrated by audit studies in which white and minority or male and female job seekers are given similar resumes and sent to the same of firms to apply for a job. These studies often find that employers are less likely to interview or offer a job to a minority or female application. Law and custom separate work-related injuries and illnesses, those caused wholly or in part by exposures to risk on the job, from physical and mental illness due to non-job causes. That distinction, however, is breaking down. As new perspectives emerge, worker rights to privacy may conflict with employer's legitimate needs to be sure that workers can function competently and safely in their jobs.

Challenges Ahead

In a tight job market today, the things that used to work may not necessarily work today. Employees are beginning to think of economic incentives as almost rights that rewards. In a recent study, "the most employees identified the top motivating techniques that they consistently did not receive. Among the respondents, 58 percent had never received personal thanks from a supervisor, 76 percent had never received written thanks, 78 percent had never been promoted for excellent performance, 81 percent had not received public praise" (Industrial Report, 2000). Another report suggests that "the companies that are not the most successful at managing high employee growth typically do not focus their efforts in recruitment, career development, culture orientation and communication." (PricewaterhouseCoopers, 2000).

Another area of improvement is the leadership. Most organizations understand that culture in their firm's cascades down from leadership and that employees emulate the behaviors leaders' model. Lack of leadership and the leadership visibility and personal interaction with other employees make it very difficult for an organization to succeed. Motivation as a form of business and human resource development can be tailored into greater productivity for many organizations. Organizations do not recognize the value of motivating their employees through incentives and rewards. Lack of employee's motivation results in poor quality.

Many organizations spend up to 10 times as much on technology as they do on work-force training. Less tangible skills are also vital such as communication, and the ability to develop positive relationship with co-workers. Lack of training programs and needs assessments cause for much organization to fail. Performance problems are traceable to many factors. Among them, lack of working tools and equipment, lack of training, lack of information, lack of policies, lack of planning, poor supervision, lack of clear work standards or expectations, rewards that do mot match the desired results, lack of feedback, lack of individual motivation, and ill defined jobs or poorly structured organizational reporting relationship. Most of these problems can be resolved by training and human resource development.

Many workers do not meet performance expectations because they were never clearly told what the expectations were or who they were supposed to meet them. Most businesses do not spend adequate time or effort developing their leaders at all levels.

To be effective, human resource development professionals must be able to meet the challenges facing organizations in the millennium and beyond. These challenges include changing workforce demographics, competing in a global economy, eliminating the skill gap, meeting the need for lifelong learning and become a learning organization.

Human Resource Development

Nadler's (1989) definition touches upon this understanding of adult development when he provided the following definitions: "learning [is] for growth of the individual, but not related to a specific present or future job (....) Development is designed to help individuals grow, through learning in general, not necessarily in a specific direction" (pp. 22-23).

Many large companies have developed sophisticated, integrated training and development programs aimed at keeping their workers apace with those of the competition. The large corporate model of the future will adopt a decentralized, location-specific system of training and recruitment, allowing individual divisions and on-site work teams to develop their own training curricula to best suit their needs. Organization may be running an extensive training facility or managing outsourced training programs developed specifically for the company by a training supplier. Organization should be working with partner companies, vendors, suppliers, and customers to acquire, train, and retrain employees. They will also find themselves on the firing line, increasingly called upon to provide demonstrable performance improvement as a result of training investment.

High-flyer programs are fast-track career-development programs for managers identified as having high potential and designated for rapid advancement in their organizations (Cox and Cooper, 1988). Many organizations want to identify high potential employees or high-flyers in order to accelerate their competence building; this is typically done by putting selected individuals on a fast track. Gibbons (1996, p. 17) refers to fast track as a "serial correlation in promotion rates," and pointed to some of the key characteristics of the concept: the multiplicity of jobs held, the relationship between them, and hierarchical progression and rapid promotions. In a strict sense, there is no substantive difference between fast-track programs and other development programs for employees, but the intensity and formality of the training activities, the selectivity regarding who is permitted to enroll, and the elitist perspective on the development process make high-flyer programs distinct. Since participants in fast-track programs are often fairly young, they serve an important role in the socialization of newcomers to the organizational culture. "The assumption is not only that the early career years of high-potential workers are years in which they will be willing, able, and eager to put high energy into their work but also that this is the best way to develop and assess potential leaders and put them on the fast-track." (Fletcher, 1996, p. 110).

According to Maslow (1943) theory on human needs, he writes "people can be motivated by non-economic incentives (…) human needs are arranged in terms of lesser to greater potency and strength and under conditions of equal deprivation, the pre-potent needs are the most urgent and persistent." (p. 5). (Read "Basis for Motivation and Change" by Robert DuPrey Ph.D.). Theories like Maslow's serve to reinforce the notion that the varied needs and desires of workers can become important sources of motivation in the workplace.

Beckhard (1969) and Alderfer (1977) define organization development as "the process of enhancing the effectiveness of an organization and the well being of its members through planned interventions that apply behavioral science concepts." (p. 10). The roles of the human resource development professional that are involved in organizational development intervention are to function as a change agent. Facilitating change often requires consulting with and advising line managers on strategies that can be used to effect the desired change. The human resource development professional may become directly involved in carrying out the intervention strategy such as facilitating a meeting of the employees responsible for planning and implementing the actual change process.

Motivation is one of the key internal factors that influence employee behavior. Motivation is defined as the psychological processes that cause energizing, direction and persistence of voluntary behavior. Theories of motivation use different sources to explain behavior, including needs theory by Maslow (1943), two-factor theory on basic needs by Herzberg (1966) and cognitive evaluation theory by Deci (1975). Each of these theories has implications for development and conducting human resource programs. Herzberg et al. (1966) claims that "people have two sets of basic needs, one focusing on survival and another focusing on personal growth (…) factors in the workplace that satisfy survival needs or hygiene factors, cannot of themselves provide job satisfaction, they only prevent dissatisfaction. Alternatively, motivator factors which satisfy the growth needs can create feelings of job satisfaction, but their absence will not lead to dissatisfaction." (p. 31). Based on Herzberg two-factor theory, workers can be motivated by ensuring that hygiene factors are present, thereby preventing dissatisfaction and then adding motivator factors to create job satisfaction.

Deci et al. (1978) cognitive evaluation theory is based on theory of motivation. He explains why incentives and rewards do not always increase motivation and performance. According to his theory, the key factor in whether rewards will be beneficial is the individual's perception of the rewards. Cognitive evaluation theory states "rewards have two aspects, information and control. When employees perceive a reward as providing information about their performance, the reward increases the employee's feelings of having control over their own actions. This enhances internal motivation, which will ensure that performance will continue. When employees perceive the reward as something being used by others to control their behavior, the reward increases the employee's feelings that they are being manipulated by the reward giver. This decreases internal motivation which may lead the employees to decrease their performance or perform the particular behavior only when reward is present." (p. 36).

Many human resource development programs and processes including training evaluation, management development and organizational development either focus on modifying employee attitude or use attitudes as a central component. Fishbein & Ajzen (1975) write that "an attitude represents a person's general felling of favorableness or unfavorable toward some stimulus object." (p. 216). Attitudes are always held with respect to a particular object, whether the object is a person, place, event, or idea, and indicate one's feelings or affect toward that object. Attitudes also tend to be stable over time and are difficult to change (Staw & Ross, 1985). Attitudes are an important factor in human resource development programs. Noe (1986) writes "two types of attitudes, reaction to skills assessment feedback and career and job attitudes can have a direct effect on the motivation to learn (…) these factors do in fact influence motivation and learning in a training program." Based on these results, Noe et al. modified the original model and suggests that "job involvement and career planning can have a significant impact on pertaining motivation and motivation to learn."

An organization's culture can also have a strong effect on individual behavior. Organizational culture is a set of values, beliefs, norms, artifacts and patterns of behavior that is shared by organization members and is used to understand and guide behavior (Ott, 1989). Individuals who understand an organization's culture are better able to accurately interpret organizational events, know what is expected of them and behave in appropriate ways in novel or unfamiliar situations. Organizations that have a string culture try to perpetuate the culture by selecting individuals who already share the culture and by socializing new members so that they accept these norms and values.

Needs Assessment

Needs assessment is a process by which an organization's human resource development needs are identified and articulated (DeSimone, 1998, p. 97). Some refer to this need as resource assessment. DeSimone et al. writes that "needs assessment is a study that can be used to identify

1) An organization's goals and its effectiveness in reaching these goals,

2) Discrepancies between employee's skills and the skills required for effective job performance,

3) Discrepancies between current skills and the skills needed to perform the job successfully in the future and

4) The conditions under which the human resource development activity will occur." (p. 97).

Needs can exist at any level, especially at the organization level, at the job and at the individual level. To ensure an effective human resource development effort, needs must be measured on each level. As a result, these type of assessments must be conducted at "organizational analysis, task analysis and person analysis (...) organizational analysis suggests where in the organization training is needed and under what conditions it will occur, task analysis explains what must be done to perform a job successfully and personal analysis reveals who needs to be trained and what kind of training they need." (McGehee & Thayer, 1961).

Needs assessment at the organization level is usually conducted by performing an organizational analysis. Organizational analysis is a process used to better understand the characteristics of the organization to determine where training and human resource development efforts are needed and the conditions within which they will be conducted. (DeSimone, 1998, p. 101). In identifying the areas that can benefit from training, the focus will be on determining which tasks and capabilities should be included in human resource development programs. Ratings of tasks on importance, time spent and ease of acquisition and rating of knowledge, skills and abilities on importance, difficulty to learn and opportunity to acquire them on the job should be examined.

Person analysis is directed at determining the training needs of the individual employee. The focus is typically on how well each employee is performing key job tasks. Person analysis is best performed by someone with the opportunity to observe the employee's performance regularly. Herbert and Doverspike (1990) point out that conditions for conducting performance appraisal and person analysis are often less than idea and they have identified the following as potential problems: "1) There can be enormous costs and complexity when considered at an organization-wide level, 2) the ability of the manager to make accurate judgments is questionable given evidence of rating errors and causal attritional biases, 3) the behavior rating system must include all areas of required performance that can be identified, 4) intentions to use performance appraisal data for needs analysis must be specified before the system is developed, operational and implemented, 5) raters must be motivated to make accurate performance ratings and 6) the manager or training director must be able to match deficiencies identified to specific remedial activities." (p. 255).

In general, the need assessment is a phase in training process and is performed on organization, task and person. In many cases due to the fact that limited human resource development professionals are available, it is necessary to prioritize training needs and needs assessment early on. This process ensures that resources have the greatest impact on the organizational goals. Whenever possible, individuals should be encouraged to participate in prioritizing needs and conduct initial assessment.

Learning & Design

DeSimone (1998) explains that "learning is defined as a relatively permanent in behavior, cognition or affect that occurs as a result of one's interaction with the environment." (p. 57). The focus of learning is change, either by acquiring something new or modifying something that already exists. The change must be long lasting before one can say learning has really occurred. The focus of learning can include behavior, affect or cognition or all three. Learning outcomes can be skill based, cognitive or affective. Learning results from an individual's interaction with the environment. Learning does not include behavior changes attributable to maturation or a temporary condition.

The definition of learning makes it clear that people acquire and develop skills, knowledge and behavior as a result of an interaction between forces within the learner and in the environment (DeSimone, 1998, p. 61). Trainability is concerned with the readiness to learn, combining trainee's levels of ability and motivation (Maier, 1973) with their perceptions of the work environment (Noe, 1986). Noe et al. (1986) has created a formula that illustrates a trainee must have both the motivation and the ability to learn.

"Trainability = f (Motivation x Ability x Perceptions of the Work Environment).

If either of the factors in the formula is lacking, learning will not occur." (Noe, 1986). The equation also shows that a very high level of one can not completely overcome a very low level of the other. Noe et al. (1986) further explains that "if employees perceive little support in the work environment for learning new knowledge or skills, they will be less likely to learn and use them."

Trainability is an important factor in human resource development. Placing employees in programs they are not motivated to attend or are not prepared to do well can waste time and resources. Trainees with less ability take longer to learn, which can increase the length of the training period and the expense involved in conducting training. Trainability testing is one approach that can be used to ensure that trainees have the motivation and ability to learn. This approach focuses on measuring the motivation and relevant abilities of candidates for training and selecting for training only those who show a sufficient level of trainability. Tubiana & Ben-Shakhar (1982) develop a questionnaire that measure motivational and personality factors to predict success in combat training. "The questionnaire measures such things as independence, sociability and motivation to serve in a combat unit. The combination of questionnaire responses and other predictors proved to be highly correlated with training success." (Tubiana & Ben-Shakhar, 1982).

Another approach to trainee testing is to allow candidates to complete part of the training program and use their performance on that section as a predictor of how well they will perform throughout the remainder of the training (Robertson & Downs, 1979).   Training design is also important in learning. Training design involves adapting the learning environment to maximize learning. Training design issues include the conditions of practice that affect learning and the factors that affect retention of what is learned.

Another perspective on the learning process and how to maximize learning examines what people do when they learn. Kolb (1984) a leading theorist on experiential learning, argues that "the learning process is not the same for all people. Because of the complex nature of the learning process, there are opportunities for individual differences and preferences to emerge (….) some people just step up and hit the ball without bothering to look very carefully at where their shot went unless it went in the pocket. Others seem to go through a great deal of analysis and measurement but seem a bit hesitant on the execution. Thus there seem to be distinctive styles or strategies for learning and playing the game." (p. 66).

Kolb theorizes that learning styles are developed as a result of life experiences, both past and present and hereditary influences. He also notes that while individuals may have a dominant learning style, they may also use other learning styles in certain situations. Kolb et al. (1984) has developed self-descriptive questionnaire that is called Learning Style Inventory, which assesses an individual's orientation toward many different modes of the learning process. His theory and the learning style inventory's theory can help human resource development professionals, supervisors and employees to identify and appreciate the number of different approaches to learning. As a result, training and development programs can be tailored to individual learner preferences in both programs and in those using computerized instruction.

Another theory that helps employees learn is Gagne-Briggs (1984) theory of instruction. His theory focuses on the kinds of things people learn and how they learn them. The theory argues that fundamentally different learning outcomes are learned in different ways. Gagne et al. (1972) proposes that "human performance can be divided into five distinguishable categories, each of which requires a different set of conditions for maximizing learning, retention, and transfer. 1) Intellectual skills, 2) Verbal information, 3) Cognitive strategies, 4) Motor skills, and 5) attitudes." (p. 384). The motor skills are being referred to using bodies to manipulate and the skills in learning by practicing the movement and in doing so the quality of the movement is improved.

According to Gagne et al. (1984) these five categories exist because "they differ, first as human performance, second, because the requirements for their learning are different despite the pervasiveness of such general conditions as contiguity and reinforcement and third because the effects of learning, the continued learning, appear also to differ from each other." (p. 384). His theory provides a good source of ideas for human resource development professionals who are looking for ways to enhance the effectiveness of their training programs.

In general, understanding the learning process and how learning can be maximized are critical issues in designing and implementing human resource development programs. Learning is defined as a relatively permanent change in behavior or cognition that occurs as a result of one's interaction with the environment. Traditional research on the learning process has identified some principles of learning such as contiguity, the law of effect and practice. Although these principles enhance understanding of the learning process, they are not sufficient for designing programs to maximize learning. Trainee characteristics play a significant role in the learning process too. Trainability is a combination of motivation and ability. The higher the level of trainability the more likely it is that the trainee will learn. Knowledge of training design in particular the conditions of practice can be used to maximize learning. Trainee learning can be improved by over learning, feedback and practice sessions spaced over time with sufficient rest periods between them.

The information or skills an employee learns are of little value to the organization if the employee does not retain or use them back on the job. Retention of what is learned is influenced by the meaningfulness of material, the degree of original learning and interference. In providing training, trainers and HR people have assessed learning needs, designed, developed and delivered training, and evaluated training results, all the activities associated with delivering an effective training program.

Overall, the main thrust of the business and departmental training objectives is to train employees, make employees competent and therefore gain commitment from employees. There has been significant training as a result of major capital investment in new and high technology equipment, as well as a very bold venture to introduce team-working between traditionally separate working groups.

A training need analysis is carried out to determine what type, level and range of training is required. The process is such that each employee is appraised at least once a year by his supervisor/training owner, and any training or development needs relevant to the individual's personal development or those required by the business are mutually agreed. This is then recorded on computer. If the training is as a consequence of capital investment in new equipment, the training needs analysis has to consider very carefully the introduction of new technology, its effect on working practices and whether employee skills and knowledge are appropriate.

If the training initiative is aimed at changing attitudes and therefore behaviors as in the introduction of team working, the training need analysis has to consider the behavior, values and psychological make-up of groups and individual employees. After considering all the factors pertaining to any training initiative, the analysis is turned into a training plan showing who is to be trained, on what and by which date. At this stage, budgets are determined, training solutions sought or devised and training providers secured. Monitoring and control of the plan is through the departmental training committee, which regularly reviews training activity, ensuring progress is maintained and training plans are fully implemented. Outcomes of training are determined by a thorough and rigorous evaluation process, which measures initial objectives against changes in behavior and performance.

Advanced technology drives the necessity to develop sophisticated training programs. With the constant push to develop modern solutions for new equipment and the progression to full automation, training needs change rapidly. The finishing end development comprises not only equipment automation but also the introduction of full tracking and routing computer packages. This involves developing training via the computer, and one such technique is the ability to build up a logic diagram to train in a step-by-step approach. Early indications are that individuals learning computer techniques for the first time are capable of making the required changes in skills.

In order to maximize the skills of teams, training initiatives will have to be developed which ensure individuals can improve by self-development and on merit. This will mean the continual development of computer packages aimed at individual learning, both at work and in the home. The use of individuals creating their own goals and incorporating them into their own training plan needs to be developed further.

With the advent of team working, the new team leaders will have to become coaches and trainers to ensure skill levels are maintained and improved. Therefore, the team leaders' abilities need to be developed by training to handle this responsibility. With technology, especially automation, industries have to learn the lesson of seeking new, innovative ways of teaching high technology with existing employees. It is mainly centered on logic diagrams and having the ability to build a pattern to understand the interactions of all components. With the creation of flatter structures within the industry, opportunities will be there for all employees within the organization to learn and expand the knowledge. With the traditional in-house training approach being complemented by much more professional training packages, everyone will benefit the individual and the business.

In the early years in an organization, training and developing people is carried out almost exclusively on the job with no training staff. When new employees are hired, their immediate supervisors are required to train them in whatever skills they need on the job. In some organizations, this situation continues even as they grow much larger. Yet, most companies of any size eventually reach the point where management recognizes it would be an economical move to provide a staff to help line manager's train and develop their people. The limitations of on-the-job training are apparent when a company is growing rapidly or turnover is high; most line managers simply don't have the time to do the training. Furthermore, many managers make poor instructors. Line managers become qualified for their positions for reasons other than their teaching ability. It may take a great deal longer for new employees to become proficient and productive on the job if they rely on line managers alone to train employees.

According to Weiss (1999) "a well-organized training department can provide several advantages to the company. A formal training group can augment the on-the-job coaching of supervisors while also contributing to the training function." He continues that "creating a training department that can research the training needs of employees to establish a more certain basis for determining the type and scope of training that should be given. It can keep up-to-date with the latest techniques and what other companies are doing. Its research activities can include investigating the value of video training programs and the availability of consulting services (…) the training staff can develop new programs and training techniques suitable to meet the training needs that have been identified through research." (pp. 5-9). Members of the training department are undoubtedly in a better position than any outside training organization to relate training programs more directly to the work environment in the company. This program development applies especially to first-level managers. At that managerial level, where the largest supervisory population exists, the economics and advantages of in-house training are favorable. The teaching and instructing role is the primary function of the training department for most companies. When the department has its own group of seminar lenders, it can be very flexible in conducting training programs that bring about desired on-the-job behavior change. Special training sessions can be scheduled and presented on short notice, and ongoing training programs can be staffed much more economically with department people than by using outside consultants.

A training department is in an ideal position to constantly evaluate the effectiveness of its programs because results can be easily and quickly ascertained by observing and testing trainees. Thus, seminar leaders can try different ways to teach different subjects, and make changes and improvements as necessary. Furnishing service and making recommendations to top-and middle-level managers on all aspects of training needs and methods is a further benefit provided by a training department. Weiss (1990) writes "generally accepted management theory makes line managers responsible for the training and development of their people. But this is with the understanding the training department can be called upon for advice and assistance." (pp. 5-9). Managers may occasionally request advice and/ or help in setting up development plans for individual employees or want to know how training can facilitate a major operational change.

Training Programs and Evaluations

"Training is for the good of plant production, it is a way to solve production problems through people, it is specific and helps people to acquire skills through the use of what they learned" (cited in Swanson & Torraco, 1995, p. 2). One of the first things a human resource development professional should do is to define the training program objectives. Mager (1984) defines an objective as a "description of a performance you want learners to be able to exhibit before you consider them competent." (p. 3). Program objectives describe the intent and the desired result of the human resource development and training program. The results can be achieved in many ways such as lectures, role play and coaching. Program objectives that lack the performance, conditions and criteria are often ambiguous and can cause those who interpret the objectives differently to feel frustrated and come into conflict with one other. It is necessary to specify observable behaviors that indicate an unobservable outcome is achieved (Mager, 1984). Mager et al. (1984) notes that "simply presenting trainees with objectives for learning or performance may be enough to elicit the desired behavior." (p. 3). Many workers do not meet performance expectations because they were never clearly told what the expectations were or who they were supposed to meet them. Clear objectives provide this information and represent the organization's expectations, which can play a key role in employee performance.

Usually after the supervisor or human resource development professional has identified the program objectives, a series of decision must be made regarding the development and delivery of the training program. One of those decisions is whether to design the program internally or purchase it from an outside vendor. One method of providing the training program is to have a trainer design and deliver the program internally. Once the organization has made a decision to design its own training program, a trainer must be selected that can deliver and has the knowledge and varied skills to design and implement a training program. Effective trainers must be able to communicate their knowledge clearly, use various instructional techniques, have good interpersonal skills and have the ability to motivate others to learn.

Training program objectives are also necessary for pinpointing outcomes of a training or human development programs, but these statements alone are insufficient for determining the content of the training program. Once the training program is designed, organizations need to select a method of training. In many cases computer-based training can be implemented using a computer at an employee's desk or at his or her workplace, in a company classroom or even at an employee's home. Other training methods are on-the-job training and classroom training or role-playing. In classroom training method, a classroom can be any training space set away from the work site, such as the company cafeteria or a meeting room. While many organizations capitalize on whatever usable space they have available to conduct training sessions, some larger organizations maintain facilities that serve as freestanding training centers. On-the-job training method involves conducting training at a trainee's regular workplace. This is the most common form of training that most employees receive at least some training and coaching on the job. Virtually any type of one-on-one instruction between coworkers and between the employee and supervisor can be classified as on-the-job training. Much of this training is conducted informally, without structure or planning or careful though. Research suggests that informal on-the-job training "leads to increased error rated, lower productivity and decreased training efficiency." (Jacobs & Jones, 1995, p. 19).

Role-playing is a very popular training method. Role-playing is reported used by 55 percent of organizations (Industry Report, 1996). In the role-playing technique, trainees are presented with an organizational situation assigned a role or character in the situation and asked to act out the role with one or more other trainees. The role-play should offer trainees an opportunity for self-discovery and learning. Another training method is Intelligent Computer-Assisted Instruction that is very flexible and has the ability to quantitatively evaluate leaner performance. According to McCalla & Greer (1977) Intelligent Computer-Assisted Instruction "patiently offers advices to individual learners encourages learner practice and stimulate learner's curiosity through experimentation. This would potentially make the teacher more available for more creative endeavors, or for helping learners to overcome subtle or difficult problems beyond the capability of Intelligent Computer-Assisted Instruction." (p. 74).

Increasing technology in processes, control systems and industrial operations, combined with the aging of the technical workforce, has called attention to the need for training of technical employees in many companies. Years ago, training was seen as the answer to a recurring problem in the workplace, or an old-timer explaining to a new hire how to repair a machine. But with today's complex equipment and instrumentation, much of what is computerized; training has become a continuing and never-ending task. Many companies are realizing the consequences of inadequately trained employees may result in poor quality products, machine and equipment downtime, and general inefficiency. As a result, training is playing a greater role and has become an important element in improving productivity and keeping manufacturing costs at a minimum.

There is probably nobody in a given organization that knows how the machine processes and control systems should work better than the long-service technicians. These people have kept the equipment and controls up and running for years. They know where every sensor, actuator and relay is located, what these controls and devices are designed to do, and how they should be operating. Weiss et al. (1999) writes "organizations cannot afford to let the mechanical skills these veterans possess be lost. They must not let these people become liabilities because of their possible resistance to or likely ignorance of new technology. Most of them may lack knowledge of new equipment that is computer-based. Before organizations get involved in a training program, however, they should assess the employees' current skill levels and aptitudes. This helps determine how much training they need and how much they can swallow. Organizations should to avoid training people on matters that aren't part of their jobs, or teaching them something they already know." (pp. 5-9)

Cross-training is another option for efficiency. Although cross-training employees to do one another's job require managers and subordinate's time, in the long run, the company will benefit. The ultimate ideal situation which can occur is that most hourly employees and many of the salary employees can do someone else's job as well as others can. The advantages of cross training are that more employees become aware of the workflow and can anticipate problems or requirements in other areas. Some employees over come the feeling they are in dead-end jobs without improving their skills. Employees can be moved around to handle peak loads in busy areas, thus improving productivity of the department.

The most important function of human resource development is that of evaluation. Kumar & Treadwell (1998) write that "evaluation must concern all HRD functions, including the work system, role analysis, annual objectives, career system, development training system, culture system, identity and ethos building, communication and reward systems, and self-renewal system, diagnosis and interventions in areas such as role efficacy and organizational climate and empowerment." (p. 802). The process of evaluation must not be considered as strict scrutiny of the books of accounts and an exercise of fault finding. Evaluation processes must be examined to see if they are objective, useful, and valid. Evaluations should be typically conducted proactively, rather than reactively, for the purposes of instituting improvements through specially designed intervention or training programs for building a culture of trust, risk-taking, and creativity on a long-term basis for all employees, both administrators and workers. The HRD audit must be conducted as a participative exercise to include workers as well as all levels of management. A variety of both qualitative and quantitative tools need to be used. Tools such as interviews, questionnaires, group discussions and workshops, observations, analysis of records, documents, and analyses of secondary source data. Such evaluations must be comprehensive, covering the HRD functions related to the work, career, training, culture, and self-renewal systems.

Human resource development and training evaluation is defined as "the systematic collection of descriptive and judgmental information necessary to make effective training decisions related to the selection, adoption, value and modification of various instructional activities." (Goldstein, 1980, p. 237). When conducting an evaluation booth descriptive and judgmental information may be collected. Descriptive information provides a picture of what is happing or has happened, whereas judgmental information communicates some opinion or belief about what has happened. Evaluation also involves the systematic collection of information according to a predetermined plan or method to ensure that the information is appropriate and useful. Evaluation is conducted to help managers, employees and human resource development professionals to make informal decisions about particular training programs and methods.

Kirkpatrick (1994) articulates that "training efforts can be evaluated according to any or all of four criteria: reaction, learning, job behavior and results." Positive reaction to a training program may make it easier to encourage employees to attend future programs. But if trainees did not like the program or think they did not learn anything, they may discourage others from attending and may be reluctant to use the skills or knowledge obtained in the program. Measuring whether someone has learned something in training may involve a quiz or test and clearly a different method from assessing the participant's reaction to the program.

The results of the training criteria are also important to training success. If learning does not transfer to the job, the training effort can not have an impact on the employee's or organization's effectiveness. It is also most challenging to assess the results of the training. Given that many things beyond employee performance can affect organizational performance such as economic and operating data that may affect the results.

Kirkpatrick's et al. model provides a useful way of looking at the possible consequences of training and reminds human resource development professionals that the efforts often have multiple objectives.

Training History

There have been many historical events that contributed to the establishment of human resource development. Many of the earlier training programs focused on skilled training. Human resource development is part of a larger human resource management system that includes training and development, career development and organization development programs and processes. Many human resource development managers and staff have to establish working relationships with line managers in order to coordinate training programs and processes throughout the organization. To be effective, Human resource development professionals need to be able to serve in many ways in order to meet the challenges facing organizations in the coming years and beyond. They may have to deal with changing workforce demographics, competing in a global economy, eliminating the skill gap, meeting the need for lifelong learning and becoming a learning organization.

Because human resource development programs are attempts to change employee behavior, it is important to understand the factors that influence employee behavior. Motivation is one of the key internal factors that influence employee's behavior. Attitudes and the employee's knowledge, skills and abilities are also important internal factors of behavior.

Understanding the learning process and how learning can be maximized are critical issues in designing and implementing training and development programs. The information or skills an employee learns are of little value to the organization of the employee does not retain or use them back on the job.

Training and human resource development needs assessment is performed on many levels. Some of the important levels are organization, task and person. Organizational level asks whether organization needs training and under what condition will the training be conducted. Task assessment level deals with job description, identifying tasks within the job, and identifies the areas than can benefit from training. Person analysis level determines who needs the training and development needs of employees. Because of limited resources it is important to prioritize training needs to ensure that resources have the greatest impact on the organizational goal.

After an organization identifies a need for training, the next step is to decide whether to purchase the program from an outside vendor or design the training program in-house. If the organization decides to stay in-house, the trainer must be selected. The trainer should have the skill, knowledge and communication skills to conduct the training or train the trainers. Once the trainer designs the training program, the next step is to determine the best schedule while avoiding potential conflict. The final step is the actual implementation of the training program.

One of the important phases in training process is evaluation. The purpose of the training evaluation is to determine whether the training program has achieved their objectives, and to build credibility and support programs to value the training. Data collection is central to the training evaluation. Some of the data collection methods in evaluating the training programs are interview, survey, observation, archival data, tests and simulations.

The levels of illiteracy within the workforce have created a demand for basic skills programs. The Computer of these programs focuses on improving basic competencies, including reading, writing and computation skills. Technical training programs may include programs in computers, technical skills, safety and quality. Computer training typically involves both on-the-job and classroom training. Technical skills and programs are generally job-specific and are offered organization-wide. Quality and team training programs are typically part of a larger quality improvement agenda and may include training needed for the organization to become ISO 9000 registered.

While the individual is ultimately responsible for his or her own career, the organization can assist the individual by providing information, opportunities and assistance. By doing so, the organization can enhance its internal labor market and be more effective in recruiting and motivating employees. Organizations use a variety of tools and techniques to manage employee careers. These include self-assessment tools and activities such as workbooks, workshops and computer programs, individual career counseling, job placement, organizational potential assessment and development programs such as job rotation and mentoring. These activities and practices will help employees gather information to develop career awareness and career plans and offer opportunities to implement plans.

Management development is also a big part of overall resource development. DeSimone (1998) writes there are "two approaches to leadership development (…) Leader Match and transformational leadership training." (p. 433). He continues "options for management education include college and university degree programs and executive education (….) based training and experience methods including courses and programs, corporate academies and on-the-job experience." (p. 433).

In organizational development and change, organizations need to use organizational transformation interventions that deal with cultural changes, learning organization and high-performance work systems. These approaches are very complex and need to be managed from the top of the organization. Cultural change and diversity at workplace is becoming more global and the need for cross-cultural training has grown drastically. DeSimone et al. (1998) writes "Valuing differences or diversity training attempts to deal with the underlying values and attitudes that manifest themselves in sexism and racism." (p. 503).

If the talent, energy and resourcefulness of hundreds of millions of men and women are not redirected to constructive ends, civilization will probably continue to disintegrate into a state of increasing destitution and lawlessness from which there may be no easy return. For this reason, finding an alternative to formal work in the marketplace is the critical task ahead for every nation on earth. Preparing for a post-market era will require far greater attention to the building up of the third sector and the renewal of community life. " Social economy unlike the market economy, which is based solely on productivity and therefore amenable to the substitution of machines for human input, the social economy is centered on human relationships, on feelings of intimacy, on companionship, fraternal bonds and stewardship, qualities not easily reducible to or replaceable by machines." (Rifkin, 1995, pp. 247-257). Because it is the one realm that machines can not fully penetrate or subsume, it will be by necessity the refuge where the displaced workers of the third Industrial Revolution will go to find renewed meaning and purpose in life after the commodity value of their labor in the formal marketplace has become marginal or worthless.

The path to a successful change journey is associated with systematic change processes that undermine transformation efforts. Some of the recommended stages in making a new workplace and building on the job paradigm may include;

1) Everyone must be considered as a contingent worker, not just the part-time and contract workers. Everyone's employment is contingent on the results that the organization can achieve.

2) Recognizing the turbulence in the business environment, workers need to regard themselves as people whose value to the organization must be demonstrated in

each   successive   situation   they   find
themselves in.

3) In the light of their contingency, workers
    need to develop a mindset, an approach to
    their work, and a way of managing their
    own careers that is more like that of an
    external vendor than that of a traditional
    employee. Workers must be wise to think
    that they are in business for themselves
    and that their tasks have been outsourced
    to them by the organization.

4) In its own interests, the wise company
    must work with these new-style workers
    collaboratively to make the relation as
    beneficial to them as possible, but the
    benefits of this new work arrangement will
    be different from the old ones. They need
    to inhere in the nature of the work itself
    rather than being add ons, like sick leave,
    guaranteed pensions and free health care.

5) Workers must act like people in business for themselves by maintaining a plan for career-long self-development, by taking primary responsibility for investing in health insurance and retirement funds and by renegotiating their compensation arrangements with the organization when and if organizational needs change.

6) Because more and more of the organization's efforts are likely to be undertaken by project teams made up of individuals from different functional backgrounds, workers must be able to switch their focus rapidly from one task to another, to work with people with very different vocational training and mindsets, and to work in situations where the group is the responsible party and the manager is only a coordinator, and to work without

clear job descriptions and to work on several projects at the same time.

7) Just as workers will need to be ready to shift from project to project within the same organization, they should expect that much more frequently than in the past they will have to move from one organization to another. Long-term employment should be for most workers, a thing of the past. "The organization must try to minimize these shifts, recognizing that they are difficult and disruptive to the effectiveness of both the organization and the worker. But both parties will have to make their long-term plans with the likelihood of such shifts in mind." (Bridges, 1994, pp. 50-51).

8) Recognizing that these are new and difficult demands, the organization need to do its part in providing information,

training and counsel to people who are making this difficult transition from the old rules to the new rules, but ultimately it is the workers, individually, who must manage this transition in their careers and their lives.

9) The government must play a far different role in the emerging high tech era, one less tied to the interests of the commercial economy and more aligned with the interests of the social economy. Forging a new partnership between the government and third sector (volunteer work) to rebuild the social economy that could help restore civic life.

10) The government needs to engage and participate in assisting the third sector, volunteer groups, and by providing a tax deduction for every hour of volunteer time

given   to   legally   certify   tax-exempt
organizations.

We are entering a new age of global markets and
automated production. The road to near worker-less
economy is within sight. Whether that road leads to a safe
haven or a terrible abyss will depend on how well
civilization prepares for the post-market era that will follow
on the heels of the Third Industrial Revolution. "The end of
work could spell a death sentence for civilization as we have
come to know it. The end of work could also signal the
beginning of a great social transformation, a rebirth of the
human spirit." (Rifkin, 1995, pp. 288-292). The future lies in
our hands.

Future Outcome & Risks Involve

Workplaces are safer and healthier than ever before,
but both the intractable health and safety hazards of
yesterday and the unknowable hazards of tomorrow will
require continued vigilance and cooperation among

workers, employers, unions and governments. Preventing and resolving old problems and recognizing new ones early on will also require new efforts in research and development. New technologies, which can resolve many workplace health and safety concerns, can also create them. Some solutions, however, are simple ones: changing the way workers work can help reduce many workplace injuries and illnesses and training can create awareness to help recognize and avoid potential workplace hazards.

Workplaces are fairer than ever before, but much remains to be done. While woman and minorities have made advances, in educational attainment, employment, and earnings, there are still workplaces where they are not welcome, including many executive suites. "Tomorrow's work will place even more of a premium on workers with education and skills." (Herman, 1999, p.101). Employers can ill afford to shut out high performers based on race or color, disability, national origin, gender, religion or age. What is right and legal, equality of workplace opportunity is increasingly an economic necessity. Workers deserve, and employers benefit from, safe, healthful, fair and inclusive workplaces. With continued attention from and cooperation among policymakers, workers, unions and employers, Government and private sectors can build on the considerable progress of the last three decades toward a future where workplaces are safer and workers are hired, developed, and promoted based solely on their abilities.

Future employers will demand not only increased skills and high-performance workplace practices but also a more flexible workforce. Labor market experts believe that nontraditional workers, people who work in alternative arrangements such as on call workers, independent contractors, temporary help or leasing agency workers, as well as contingent workers, will be a larger share of the future workforce. According to one national study (1994), "65 percent of employers believed that, in the future, firms would increase their use of flexible staffing arrangements." The use of nontraditional workers fits with the evolving perceptions of employers regarding labor costs, competition, changing obligations, and potential litigation. Just in time workers mirror the successful industrial model of just in time inventories.

Firms wanting to become more efficient or to protect against layoffs in an economic downturn may use nontraditional staffing arrangements. Such a staffing strategy can improve a firm's competitive position by using the mix of traditional and nontraditional employees that best meets the firm's needs. However, nontraditional employees are increasingly viewed as the just-in-time workforce. These employees receive little employer-provided training and are far less likely to receive benefits through their employers. Their hiring arrangements are frequently handled by the firm's purchasing department, making for a different entry and work status on the part of the firm.

Among nontraditional workers, the number of professionals is increasing. These workers are more likely to command high wages and buy their own health and life insurance. Employers may attempt to attract these workers by increasing portability of pensions and health insurance. Although increasing in number, high-skilled professionals will remain a minority in the nontraditional workforce. A workforce composed totally of traditional workers is becoming a thing of the past. While its future proportions are still debatable, the nontraditional workforce will probably increase. At the same time, employer–employee relationships are changing. Whether one thinks about the nontraditional workforce in terms of the changing social contract, a move to just-in-time workers, or a way to make human capital flexible in a competitive global economy, the definitions of employee, employer, and workday are certainly changing, raising a number of issues. There is a growing policy division regarding the nontraditional workforce.

Some perceive this as a large and growing workforce that employers relegate to second-class employment, with no worker benefits, little or no mutual loyalty, and all risk borne by the employee, while employers benefit from lower costs. In essence, they see a strong need to contain this type of work. Others see the nontraditional workforce as an opportunity for the worker to achieve flexibility in work schedule, gain new experiences, or use as a bridge between times of full employment. This latter group sees the growth of the nontraditional work force as a win–win situation to be encouraged.

With the increase in creative staffing arrangements, including temporary help, leasing, and contract work, there may be a need to examine and possibly reformulate the definitions of employer and workplace for determining responsibility for wages and benefits as well as other standards and regulations.

It is sometimes difficult to determine whether a worker is an employee of a firm, an independent contractor, or working for a third party. Whether the employer's record keeping is purposely obscure or there is an honest mistake, workers entitled to benefits may not receive them. Worker misclassification is not an easy problem to solve and will only grow worse as more nontraditional workers join the labor force. Courts and Congress have been asked to address this issue, usually on a piecemeal basis under a specific law. As the nontraditional workforce grows, it will become even more important for the Department of Labor and other government agencies to help employers maintain proper classifications.

It is also imperative that private firms, business associations, unions, and intermediary organizations address these complex problems and find solutions that enhance workforce flexibility, while giving workers and taxpayers what they deserve. Nontraditional workers generally receive less training than do traditional workers for a number of reasons, including employees' lack of a long-term commitment. Regardless of the reason, this nation cannot afford to let any class of workers fall behind in skill development. Temporary help agencies, labor unions, nonprofit organizations, and employer groups can enhance their training of various work groups. Small businesses that lack resources can participate in sectional training or train through intermediary organizations such as temporary help agencies. Government can support such training, either indirectly through diverse organizations, or directly, as in the support now given by the Department of Labor and by the Small Business Assistance Programs in various federal agencies.

Worker benefits and protections: Non-traditional workers receive fewer benefits, be they health care, vacation, unemployment compensation, or pensions, than do full-time workers. Some of this is due to eligibility and coverage definitions, some to improper company record keeping and some simply to lack of access. These complex issues are not easily resolved. While not all-nontraditional workers will or perhaps should receive the same benefits as other workers, much can be done to help them obtain access to essential benefits. This raises challenges for corporations, small businesses, labor unions, contracting firms, and temporary help agencies on a number of fronts. Options include: increase the application of already successful models, such as portable pension plans; broaden eligibility requirements; and keep better records so that workers' potential wages and benefits can be properly ascertained. While these solutions may at first appear to be disadvantageous to employers because of their costs, to labor unions because they encourage nontraditional work, and to temporary help organizations because it reduces their competitive advantage, self-determination and cooperative ventures in fact offer some of the best solutions.

Another aspect of the changing workplace is the increasing job insecurity for some workers. Job insecurity is a concern of workers in both traditional and nontraditional work arrangements, particularly in a dynamic economy characterized by high rates of job dislocation as well as job creation. It arises from worker concern both about being displaced losing a job and about having difficulty finding another equally desirable one. Job insecurity includes both lack of job stability job change and workers' perceptions about job security. Job stability can be measured in terms of how long jobs last and whether there has been a decline in job tenure. Job security, however, is more subjective: workers may voluntarily change jobs more often when economic times are good or change jobs less often when they are more concerned about job security and see fewer opportunities. Involuntary job loss clearly provides one measure of job insecurity.

How much value do workers place on job security? While loss of a job is generally an unpleasant experience, a highly skilled and highly mobile workforce may place a lower value on job stability and may even value voluntary job change and job variety. Concern about job security probably diminishes for many workers during periods of low unemployment when the risk of long periods of unemployment is less.

Many people believe job insecurity has increased in recent years, despite low unemployment rates that would seem to indicate increasing job security. The 2009 has been marked by concern about displaced workers, those who permanently lost their jobs because their plant or company closed or moved, there was insufficient work for them to do, or their positions or shifts were abolished. In the early 2000s, several major news publications ran stories on the extent of job displacement in the U.S. workforce, with the implication that job insecurity had increased.

Yet during "1995 and 1996, employment actually rose by 5 million and the unemployment rate fell to its lowest level since the end of the 1990–1991 recession.

Nevertheless, under strong labor market conditions, workers will lose jobs. Such job churning is expected even in a strong economy. (....) the mid-1990s stories in the media about job displacement reflected the number of workers displaced during the early-1990s recession, a number certainly greater than the number who had been displaced in the late 1980s and greater still than the number displaced a decade earlier. During 1991 and 1992, 5.4 million workers were displaced; about half of them, 2.8 million, were long-tenured workers, workers who had held their jobs for three or more years." (Gardner, 1995).

Labor market recovery from "the 1990–1991 recessions were slow compared to recoveries from earlier recessions. But when economic activity accelerated in 1993 and 1994, both the level and the risk of job displacement began to fall. Between 1993 and 1994, a period of strong labor market conditions, 2.4 million long-tenured workers were displaced from their jobs, 0.4 million fewer than were displaced between 1991 and 1992. The displacement rate, which reflects the likelihood of job loss during specific periods, fell from 3.9 percent in the 1991–1992 period to 3.2 percent in 1993 to 1994." (Hipple, 1997). Bureau of Labor Statistics (BLS) data show that "during the 1995–1996 periods, the number of workers displaced fell further to 2.2 million and the displacement rate to 2.9 percent." (Hipple, 1999).

The businesses that are going to succeed in a competitive market place are those who are able to tap into leadership abilities and bright ideas of their employees at all levels. This means that in order to continually improve the bottom line, attention should be paid to the effective training of those employees who have been given the responsibility of leading others to the accomplishment of company goals. Good leadership at all levels, from the first lines supervisor to the top executive, make all companies better. Good leadership training makes effective leaders.

The training methods that must be used in training program must relate directly to organizational training objectives and the content of a particular course. If, for example, organization intend to train their employees in the procedures of operating a computer, simulation or demonstration methods will be better than lectures. Here are some suggestions on selecting training methods. Analyze the people to be trained to determine how best to do it. Assess their maturity level, skill level already attained and their work experience. This analysis will help organization decide what training approach would be most appropriate. Base the methods on the capabilities and strengths of the organization training staff, but also give the members additional training to expand their instructional skills. Consider time and cost factors. If organizations are to train a large group quickly, or have limited funds to work with, they will have to tailor their program accordingly. Organizations need to allow for the physical limitations of the training environment.

When planning and scheduling the program, take into account the availability of training rooms, the type of visual aids organization can use, and the number of productive machines and equipment which may be freed for on-the-job training. It pays to continually vary organization-training methods, if for no other reason than to prevent them from becoming boring and to maintain the interest and attention of trainees. Switch the presentation style periodically and use different ways of getting trainees involved. If the training programs are not well received, getting better results may be as simple as changing the training methods.

Investigate Performance Problems. Performance problems must be fairly investigated. There are two steps to follow to properly investigate performance problems.

First, always gather the facts before taking action. If a lawsuit is filed, the company must show that there is substantial evidence for the company to reasonably believe there is good cause to discipline or fire an employee. Thus, supervisors must fairly investigate all of the facts. This means they must speak with all of the employees involved in the incident. They should not rely on what a few employees say regarding an incident and draw conclusions without getting both sides. Thus, unless the supervisor has witnessed the event first hand, the supervisor should be on a fact-finding mission. The employee whose performance is at issue should be interviewed and no conclusions drawn until after all other employees who have knowledge of the incident are interviewed. Meet with the employees in private and if the charges are serious, have the employee give you a statement in writing. Be patient and receptive. Gather the facts without emotional involvement. Be a good listener. This shows that they understand what is being said by 1) maintaining good eye contact 2) doing nothing else while they are listening, and most importantly, 3) remembering what is being said and responding with empathy to the emotions being expressed, while restating a summary of what was said. This helps ensure that the employee perceives that the supervisor understands and respects him or her.

Determine whether the employee was adequately apprised of what was expected. For example, was there a job description or an office manual that described the job duties in detail, or was the written assignment sufficiently detailed? Did the employee sign something acknowledging having received and read the description, manual, or the assignment?

There are many ways to develop partnership to transfer managers and supervisors into performance development. Develop a strategically integrated HRD philosophy. This is accomplished by adopting a system of values and guiding principles that are performance centered. Improve organizational effectiveness. An organizational effectiveness framework, used in conjunction with strategic planning, helps identify possible breakdowns in the organization and set priorities. Create performance partnerships. Partnerships are created at these levels: strategic business partnerships that cross units or divisions; management development partnerships to transform managers and supervisors into performance coaches; and organizational development partnerships, in which HRD practitioners must have access to organizational leaders and decision makers in order to alter organizational and performance management systems. Unleash HRD practice.

This step requires adopting a new approach that connects performance improvement and change interventions to the strategic business goals of the organization and that focuses on learning transfer strategies.

Organizations need to apply tools and technology to improve HRD and the organization. Human resource development professionals need to follow certain training guidelines in order to have successful training programs. 1) Building relationships, 2) training, coaching, and mentoring, 3) confronting performance, 4) enhancing employees' self-esteem, and 5) rewarding performance.

Organizations can avoid misdiagnosing their problems by doing some homework such as , identify the stakeholders who are involved, which staff, managers, customers, or even competitors have knowledge or beating on this problem. Sometimes the first problem they see is just the tip of the iceberg. Says Laurie Simoneau, director of training for Donna Karan International Inc., "The extra effort you invest up front makes the difference between solving a real problem or just delivering a training program."

To design a training program, organizations need to go back to the original problem and define measurable outcomes. Then quantify the improvement in operation leaders want to see after training is complete. Let the original problem determine the outcomes that the organization training should achieve. The most effective program is to first train workers in new behaviors and then train managers to support employees as they apply their learning daily. Simoneau (1998) suggests "delivering the training program to managers first, or inviting managers to an executive briefing on the program so that they are enrolled in the change."

Organizations should begin any training effort with the budget and timeframe in mind. That way, they would not spend months designing a Taj Mahal, only to find later that they have the budget for a shack. In addition to budget and timeline, consider the timing of the training. Avoid busy seasons, layoff periods, upsizing and other stressful times.

Get input from all parts of the company as to what times work best for them.

Get agreement at all levels on the definition of the problem, the need for training and the training program chosen. Keep people posted on organizational training progress. Test the program before the big launch. Doing a dry run with a small group of participants will help ensure a successful program for the masses. Sometimes a good approach is to use outside trainers as consultants to help to develop an in-house program, and as an occasional change of pace to give the training a new look. External trainers can also be paired with in-house facilitators for maximum credibility and expertise. Explain a concept verbally, and then let participants get involved with the issue. For example, participants in a sales program can role-play sales calls, critiquing each other's performances. Give participants a chance to teach someone else. "The best way to learn something" says Covey (1998), "is to teach it to someone else within two days". Allow participants to discuss and learn from each other. "This is a powerful way to build relationships and teamwork between participants" says

Simoneau (1998). Allow participants to debrief. According to Silberman (1999) "It's not the games or exercises that are so important, it's the conversation that takes place after the game or exercise".

Craig Taylor (1999) of the Disney Institute also points out that training can be used to reinforce a company's culture. "Training is the lubricant that builds a strong culture, and a strong culture helps organizations weather difficult times."

The path for a successful training should be thought of as a four-phase process: Phase 1-Identify the root problem. Phase 2-Determine your training needs and choose a training program. Phase 3-Conduct the training sessions. Phase 4-Follow up the sessions with ongoing reinforcement. Reinforcement mechanisms include: Support for the new behaviors by management. Recognition of new behaviors through rewards and mentions in company newsletters, staff meetings and on bulletin boards. Reinforcement of the training messages, logos and themes in company materials. Involve participants in designing your reinforcement program for maximum effectiveness.

To motivate today's employees is to personally thank employees for doing a good job--one-on-one, in writing, or both. Leaders should take the time to meet with and listen to employees as much as they need or want. Leaders should provide specific feedback about the performance of the person, the department, and the organization. Employees and workers are striving to create a work environment that is open, trusting, and fun. Leaders of organizations should encourage new ideas and initiatives. They should to provide information on how the organization earns its revenues, upcoming products and strategies for competing in the marketplace, and how workers fit into the overall plan. Leaders of organizations must involve employees in decisions, especially those that affect them and their work. Recognize, reward, and promote people based on their work and the work environment and provide people with a sense of ownership in their work and the work environment. They need to give people a chance to grow and learn new skills, show them how he or she can help them meet their goals within the context of meeting the organization's goals. In these ways leaders create a partnership with each employee.

Unemployment is a major risk factor. In information age that we are in, more sophisticated software technologies are bringing civilization ever closer to near workless world. In the agricultural, manufacturing and service sectors, machines are quickly replacing human labor and promise an economy of near automated production by the mid-decades of the twenty-first century. The wholesale substitution of machines for workers is going to force every nation to rethink the role of human beings in the social process. Redefining opportunities and responsibilities for millions of people in a society absent of mass formal employment is likely to be the single most pressing social issue of the coming century.

Nowhere is the effect of the computer revolution and re-engineering of the workplace more pronounced than in the manufacturing sector. Many years after Marl Marx (date not known) urged "the workers of the world to unite".

Attali (1991), a French minister and technology consultant to socialist president Francois Mitterrand, confidently proclaimed "the end of the era of the working man and woman." (p. 7). Attali et al. (1991) notes that "machines are the new proletariats and the working class is being given its walking papers" (p.7).

While the industrial worker is being phased out of the economic process, many economists and elected officials continue to hold out hope that the service sector and white collar work will be able to absorb the millions of unemployed laborers in search of work. Automation and re-engineering are already replacing human labor across a wide swath of service related fields. The new thinking machines are capable of performing many of the mental tasks now performed by human beings and at greater speeds.

"The steady upward climb in unemployment, in each decade, becomes even more troubling when organizations add the growing number of part-time workers who are in search of full-time employment and the number of discouraged workers who are no longer looking for a job." (Rifkin, 1995, p.11). According to U.S. Bureau of Labor Statistics (1993), "in 1993 more than 8.7 million people were unemployed, 6.1 million were working part-time but wanted full-time employment, and more than a million were so discouraged they stopped looking for a job altogether." Peter Drucker (1993) notes that "the disappearance of labor as a key factor of production is going to emerge as the critical unfinished business of capitalist society." (p. 12).

The father of cybernetics, Weiner (1950), who perhaps more than any other human being was in a position to clearly perceive the long-term consequences of the new automation technologies, warned of the dangers of widespread and permanent technological unemployment. He writes that "if these changes in the demand for labor come upon us in a haphazard and ill-organized way, we may well be in for the greatest period of unemployment we have yet seen." (p. 84)

Other risk that Rifkin (1996) notes is occupational diseases. "While the collective success during this century has been impressive, roughly 50,000 workers still die year from occupational diseases." (p. 188). Unlike deaths due to injuries, fatalities from occupational diseases are frequently overlooked because they tend to occur long after workers are exposed to harmful chemical or physical agents. The latency period, the time between exposure to a hazardous chemical and the onset of disease, may be decades long. "In Europe, the unemployment problem is likely to be further exacerbated by the drop in public employment. During the 1980s, public sector job, totaling 5 million, accounted for most of the job growth in the European Union." (Times, 1993, p. A1). With European nations thinning their budgets in an afford to lower government deficits and debt the prospect of governments hiring displaced manufacturing and service workers and acting as an employer of last resort is no longer politically feasible. "Even more alarming is the fact that more than 45.8 percent of the unemployed workers in Europe have been without a job for more than a year." (Report, 1993, p.37).

REFERANCES

Atkinson, D. R. and Court, H. R. (1998). The New Economic Index: Understanding America's Economic Transformation. Washington, D.C.: The Progressive Policy Institute. p. 19.

Attali, J. (1991). Millennium: winners and losers in the coming world order. New York: Random House. P. 101.

Bailey, T. (1993). Discretionary effort and the organization of work: employee participation and work reform since hawthorne. Teachers College, Columbia University. New York.

Bednarzik, W. R. (1993). An analysis of U.S. industries sensitive to foreign trade. Monthly Labor Review. Pp. 15-31.

Beniger, J. (1986). The control revolution: technological and economic origins of the information society. Cambridge, MA: Harvard University Press. Pp. 280-284.

Bowers, N. & Swaim, P. (1994). Recent trends in job training. Contemporary Economic Policy, Vol. XIII, pp. 79-88.

Bridges, W. (1994). Job shift: how to prosper in a workplace without jobs. Reading Mass: Perseus Books. Pp. 14, 67-73

Cowdrick, E. (1927). The new economic gospel of consumption. Industrial management. P. 208

Davidow, W. & Malone, M. (1992). The virtual corporation: restructuring and revitalizing the corporation for the 21st century. New York: HarperCollins.

Dohse, K., Jurgerns, U. & Malsch, T. (1985). From fordism to toyotism: the social organization of the labor process in the Japanese automobile industry. Politics and Society 14 32. Pp. 115-146.

Drucker, P. (1993). Post-capitalist society. New York: Harper Collins.

Durcker, P. (1999). Management challenges for the 21st century. New York: Harper Collins. P.135, 142

Employment Outlook (1993). Organization for economic co-operation and development. p. 20; Human Development Report, p. 37.

Employment/Unemployment Study (1993). Europeans fear unemployment will only rise. New York Times. June 13. P. A1.

Engels, F. (1946). Socialism, utopian and scientific: in ten classics of marxism. New York: International Publisher. Pp. 25,62-63.

Gardner, M. J. (1995). Worker displacement: a decade of change. Monthly Labor Review.

Gittleman, M., Horrigan, M. & Joyce, M. (1998). Flexible workplace practices: evidence from a nationally representative survey. Industrial & Labor Relations Review.

Hipple, S. (1997). Worker displacement in an expanding economy. Monthly Labor Review.

Hipple, S. (1999). Ongoing labor market strength reduces worker displacement. Monthly Labor Review.

Herman, M. A. (1999). Future work: trends and challenges for the work in the 21st century. Harvard Press. P. 209.

Judy, W. R. and D'Amico, J. (1997). Workforce 2020. Indianapolis, Indiana: Hudson Institute Inc. pp. 17-18.

King, J. (1995). High performance work systems and firm performance. Monthly labor review.

Kruse, D. (1993). Profit sharing: does it make a difference?. Upjohn, Kalamazoo, MI

Leontief, W. (1982). The distribution of work and income. Scientific American. P. 194-195.

Leontief, W. (1986). The future impact of automation on workers. New York: Oxford University Press.

Loveman, G. W. & Chris T. (1988). Good jobs or bad jobs: what does the evidence say?. New England Economic Review. January/February:46-65.

Loveman, G. (1994). An increasing bifurcation of the labor market.

Mjaedi, A. (2010). Baltimore, MD

Office of the Vice President release on the U.S. Department of Commerce report (1997). The Emerging Digital Economy II.

Platzer, D. M. (1999). Cyberstates 3.0: A State-By-State Overview of High Technology Industry. American Electronic Association.

Rifkin, J. (1996). The end of work: technology, jobs and your future. New York: Putnam Book. Pp.7, 11,101, 118,292-293.

Taylor, F. (1892). The principles and practice. Germany

Theobald, R. (1967). The guaranteed income. New York: Anchor Books. P. 19.

U.S. Bureau of Labor Statistics (1993). Current population survey

USA Today (1996). Economic anxiety.

U.S. Department of Labor (1999), Report on the American Workforce, Chapter 2—The Many Facets of Skills.

U.S. Department of Defense, Military Health System,
        Computer/Electronic. Accommodations Program. (Online)
        http://www.tricare.osd.mil/cap/accommodations/accommoda
        tion.html.
U.S. Department of Labor (1998). Bureau of Labor Statistics press
        release. Worker Displacement, p. 97. (On-line)
        http://stats.bls.gov/news.release/disp.toc.htm
Veblen, T. (1921). The Engineers and the Price System. New York:
        B.W. Huebsch. Pp. 120-121.
Wallace, M. (1989). Brave new workplace: work and occupations. Vol.
        16 #4. P. 366
Weiner, N. (1950). The human use of human beings: cybernetics and
        human beings. Boston: Houghton Mifflin.
        Zuboff, S. (1988). In the Age of the Smart Machine. New York:
        Basic Books
Callahan, M.R. (1989). Preparing the new global manager. Training and
        Development Journal, 43(3), pp. 28-32.
Carnevale, A.P. & Gainer, L.J. (1989). The learning enterprise.
        Alexandria, VA: The American Society for Training and
        Development and Washington D.C.: Government Printing
        Office.ox,
C.J. & Cooper, C.L. (1988). High-flyers. an anatomy of managerial
        success. Oxford: Basil Blackwell.
Deci, E.L., & Porac, J. (1978). Cognitive evaluation theory and the
        study of human motivation. In M.R. Lepper and D. Greene
        (Eds.), The hidden costs of rewards. Hillsdale, NJ:Lawrence
        Erlbaum Associates.
Desatnick, R.L. (1987). Building the customer-oriented work force.
        Training and Development Journal, 41(3), pp. 72-74.
DeSimone, L.R. & Harris, M.D. (1998). Human resource development.
        Pp. 32-33,258-259. Orlando, Fl.: Dryden Press
Dolanski, S. (1997). Are experts getting lost in the translation.
        Workforce, 76(2). Pp. 32-39. Journal, 44(5), pp. 17-22.
Drucker, F.P. (1999). Management challenges for the 21st century. P.
        146. N.Y.: Harper Collins Publishers.
Fiedler, F.E. (1964). A contingency model of leadership effectiveness.
        In L. Berkowitz (Ed.), Advances in experimental social
        psychology. Pp. 149-190. New York: Academic Press.
Fiedler, F.E., & Chemers, M.M. (1984). Improving leadership
        effectiveness: the leader match concept (2nd ed.). New York:

Wiley.

Fishbein, M., & Ajzen, I. (1975). Belief attitude, intention and behavior. Reading, MA:Addison-Wesley.

Fletcher, J.K. (1996). A relational approach to the protean worker. In D.T. Hall and Associates, The career is dead – long live the career: Pp. 105-131. San Francisco: Jossey-Bass.

Gagne, R.M. (1972). Domains of learning. Interchange. Pp. 3, 1-8.

Gagne, R.M. (1984). Learning outcomes and their effects: Useful categories of human performance. American Psychologist. Pp. 39, 377-385.

Gagne, R.M., & Briggs, L.J. (1979). Principles of instructional design (2nd ed.). New York: Holt, Rinehart and Winston.

Geertz, C. (1973). The interpretation of culture. New York: Basic Books.

Gephart, M.A., Marsick, V.J., Van Buren, M.E. & Spiro, M.S. (1996). Learning organizations come alive. Training & Development, 50(12). Pp. 35-45.

Gibbons, R. (196). Incentives and career in organizations. NBER Working Paper 5705. Cambridge, MA: National Bureau of Economic Research

Goldstein, I.L. (1980). Training in work organizations. Annual Review of Psychology. Pp. 31, 229-272.

Guzzo, R.A., & Dickson, M.W. (1996). Teams in organizations: recent research on performance and effectiveness. Annual review Psychology. Pp. 47, 307-338.

Hall-Sheey, J. (1985). Course design for PC training. Training and Development Journal, 39(3). Pp. 66-67.

Herbert, G.R., & Doverspike, D. (1990). Performance appraisal in the training needs analysis process: A review and critique. Public Personnel management, 19(3).pp. 253-270.

Herzberg, F.H. (1966). Work and the nature of man. Cleveland: World Publishing Co.

Jacobs, R.L. & Jones, M.J. (1995). Structured on-the-job training. San Francisco: Berrett-Koehler Publishers.

Judy, R.W. & D'Amico, C. (1997). Workforce 2020: work and workers in the 21st century. Indianapolis: Hudson Institute.

Kirkpatrick, D.L. (1994). Evaluating training programs: the four levels. San Francisco: Berrett-Koehler Publishers.

Kolb, D.A. (1984). Experiential learning. Englewood Cliffs, NJ:

Prentice-Hall.

Kumar, V.K. & Treadwell, T.W. (1998). Personnel psychology. P. 802.

Lewin, K. (1958). Group decision and social change. In E.E. Moccoby, T.M. Newcomb, and E.L. Hartley (Ed.), Reading in Social Psycology. Pp. 197-211. New York: Holt, Rinehart and Winston.

Lynch, F.R. (1997). The diversity machine: the drive to change the white male workplace. New York. The Free Press.

Mager, R.F. (1984). Preparing instructional objectives (2nd ed.). Belmont, CA Pitman Learning.

Maier, N.R.F. (1973). Psychology in industrial organizations (4th ed.). Boston: Houghton Mifflin.

Maslow, A.H. (1943). A theory of human behavior. Psychological Review. Pp. 50, 370-396.

McCalla, G.I., & Greer, J.E. (1987). The practical use of artificial intelligence in automated tutoring systems: Current status and implements to progress. Saskstoon, Canada: Princeton University Press.

McGehee, W., & Thayer, P.W. (1961). Training in business and industry. New York: Wiley.

Mitchiner, M. (2000). Leadership skills: the overlooked training. P. 10. South Carolina Business Journal.

Miller, T.O. (1992). A customer's definition of quality. Journal of Business Strategy, 13(1). P. 47.

Mueller, N. (1996). Wisconsin power and light's model diversity program.

Training & Development. Pp. 57-60.

Nadler, L. & Nadler, Z. (1989). Developing human resources. San Francisco: Jossey-Bass.

Nadler, L. (1984). Human resource development. In L. Nadler (ed.).

The handbook of human resource development. New York: John Wiley and Sons.

Noe, R. A. (1986). Trainee's attributes and attitudes: Neglected influences on training effectiveness. Academy of Management Review. Pp. 11, 736-749.

Pace, R.W., Smith, P.C., & Mills, G.E. (1991). Human resource development. Englewood Cliffs, NJ: Prentice-Hall.

Reimann, C.W. & Hertz, H.S. (1996). The baldrige award and ISO 9000 registration compared. Journal for Quality & Participation. Pp. 12-19.

Robertson, I., & Downs, S. (1979). Learning and prediction of performance: Development of trainability testing in the United Kingdom. Journal of Applied Psychology. Pp. 64, 42-50.

Schein, E.H. (1987). Coming to a new awareness of organizational culture. In E.H. Schein (Ed.), The art of managing human resources. Pp. 261-278. New York: Oxford University Press.

Senge, P.M. (1990). The fifth discipline: The art & practice of the learning organization. New York: Doubleday.

Senge, P.M. (1996). Leading learning organizations. Training & Development,50(12). Pp. 36-37

Sharma, A. (1997). Professional as agent: Knowledge asymmetry in agency exchange. Academy of Management Review. Pp. 22, 758-798.

Staw, B.M., & Ross, J. (1985). Stability in the midst of change: A dispositional approach to job attitudes. Journal of Applied Psychology. Pp. 70, 469-480.

Steck, R.N. (1992). The skills gap and how to deal with it. D&B Report, 40(1). Pp. 47-48.

Tan, D.L., Morris, L, & Romero, J. (1996). Changes in attitude after diversity training. Training & Development, 50(9). Pp. 54-55.

Thomas, R.R. Jr. (1991). Beyond race and gender. New York: Amacom.

Torraco, R.J., & Swanson, R.A. (1995). The strategic roles of human resource development. Human Resource Planning. Pp. 10-29.

Tubiana, J.H., & Ben-Shakhar, G. (1982). An objective group questionnaire as a substitute for a personal interview in the prediction of success in military training in Israel. Personnel Psychology. Pp. 35, 349-357.

Weiss, H.M. (1990). Learning theory and industrial and organizational psychology. Pp. 171-221. Palo Alto, CA: Consulting Psychologist Press.

Woodman, R.W. (1989). Organization change and development: New areas for inquiry end action. Journal of Management. Pp. 15, 205-228.